GROUNDED

Captain Emma Henderson MBE

Fisher King Publishing

GROUNDED

Published by
Fisher King Publishing
www.fisherkingpublishing.co.uk

Copyright © Captain Emma Henderson MBE 2024

Hardback ISBN: 978-1-916776-42-5
Trade Paperback ISBN: 978-1-916776-15-9
Ebook ISBN: 978-1-916776-16-6

Printed and bound by CPI Group (UK) Ltd.

MIX
Paper | Supporting
responsible forestry
FSC® C013604

For Jim, because almost everything you are
about to read was his idea for me to find my
wings again, and also, as cheesy as it sounds, he
is the wind beneath them.

For Thomas, Sophie and Megan who are the
most wonderful children a Mummy could have.

Thank you for keeping me Grounded.

I love you all.

"Life isn't always easy; it is how we overcome challenges that defines us. Emma's journey will resonate with so many in and outside of the airline industry. Above all it will leave you inspired and motivated. Brilliant read."

Mandy Hickson
First woman to fly the Tornado GR4 on the front line, leading TedX speaker and bestselling author

"This book is about a woman's journey to become an airline captain… But it delivers much, much more than just flying stories. It's about how to face your fears, how to lead, how to deal with failure, and above all how to do it all with humour and class. It epitomises how to aim high, whilst keeping your feet firmly on the ground. Devour it and learn from it!"

Sarah Furness
Best Selling author, internationally renowned speaker, former combat helicopter pilot

Acknowledgements

It takes a village to raise a child, in the same way that it takes a team to write a book, and as I have found time and time again, no one can achieve anything significant on their own.

This is certainly true of this book, and the first person who deserves to be thanked is the man who has not only shared my life for thirty years, but also my dreams, Jim. He gave me three beautiful children, built us a home, and walks with me through every valley and every mountain top. He has never stopped encouraging me, from suggesting I learn to fly again, to supporting our family when that took me away from home, holding everything together when I was building the Project Wingman team, and spending hours and hours reading, proof reading and reading again, the pages of this book. I know I cast a shadow darling, thank you for sometimes having to live in it so gracefully.

Thomas, Sophie and Megan, thank you for not laughing at me when I told you I was going to write a book, for genuinely being interested in what it would be about, and for making my job easier. A lot of this story has only happened because of sacrifices that you have had to make in allowing me to pursue a career that meant I couldn't be there to put you to bed every night as I had always planned to do. I am so proud of the adults that you have become and the plans you have for your lives. I am especially grateful for the unwavering support you gave me when I made the hardest decision of all, to leave the job I loved so much and within which I had achieved success, partly at your expense. I hope I have been able to show you in return that you can achieve your dreams and break the mould.

The two people who have always been there to celebrate my wins and carry me through the lows are also the two people who have taught me everything I know about life and set a high bar of expectation when it comes to love and generosity. Mum and Dad, you have always shown us that the reason we are here is to love each other and the excitement and encouragement you have shown as this book has grown from an idea to a reality means everything. I am so glad that I was able to fly you around Auckland, and also that I was able to fly Dad up and down from Inverness. Having my family as passengers on my aircraft is one of the biggest privileges of my career in the air, and knowing that you are always there, no matter what is happening keeps me firmly grounded. I promise to put you in a nice care home when the time comes!

To Chris and Sharelle, thank you for tolerating me as a daughter in law for so many years. Chris, you have always been so proud of me becoming a pilot and seeing what an achievement this was 12,000 miles from home and with your three small grandchildren in tow. You may not realise how much your acknowledgement of this and your pride in everything I have gone on to achieve has meant to me, so here it is in black and white. Thank you!

Our brothers, Andrew and Mark, you are both such a big part of this story. Mark, when you were kidnapped, I learned more about resilience and hope than I ever thought I would need to, and the way you dealt with the aftermath of all of that, with grace and dignity, and a big dollop of humour, has always reminded me not to get too bogged down with the little things. Andrew, you are a survivor, and watching you take on the challenge of learning to live in a wheelchair, bossing it, and becoming a world champion athlete in the process has been astonishing. Not just because you are my baby brother, but because so many people just give up, you did not.

We almost lost both of you and I literally thank God every day that we didn't. Thank you for being two such strong and loving men in my life.

As for the wider family, the Camp Milestone crew, without you there would be no book. When I first mentioned the idea of it on that first family camp back in 2020, you loved the concept and ran with it. From the moment I was absorbed into the Henderson/ Thomson clan you have treated me as one of your own. You don't just love with words and thoughts, you love with actions as well and being a part of that means that any challenge that is thrown our way can be overcome. Let's never stop laughing, or playing Mafia around the campfire!

Surrounding yourself with good people is a winning formula for life and I am surrounded by some of the best.

My best friend, the real-life Bridget Jones, thank you for never doubting me for a second and for being there even when I have been so bad at remembering birthdays and not eating chocolate. Liz and Kim, the Thursday Clubbers has not only been a mainstay of our collective sanity but been the place where I have been able to sense check ideas while we have been walking the dogs, and Lucy, likewise, but with swimming in the Moray Firth... in February. Zoe, thank you for all the brainstorming and also for proof-reading for me, and also Marnie for Angry Birds and what that has become; it was our safe place to fall in 2020 and I love the community it has turned into!

My 'pirate' friends at North London Military Wives Choir, I need to dedicate a special thank you to you. You raised me up so I could stand on mountains at a time when I was utterly lost. Together we have carried each other through highs and lows, babies have been born, we have lost people along the way, and it would be wrong to leave out our girl Jody who never got to see this book published, although I know she would have loved reading it, in her flip flops and dryrobe! The fun we all had together is what has made us stronger (see what I did there) and Rachael and Jo - thank you for not only never minding my bad behaviour but encouraging it! I love you both and I love what MWC does to bring us all together no matter where we are posted.

Charlie and Sue, thank you for being constantly encouraging and full of enthusiasm. Sue, you are responsible for me getting the job at easyJet - so thank you for starting that journey off, and Charlie, thank you for believing in me so much that you gave me my first Captain rank slides, I still have them.

Similarly, thank you Mike for noticing that I was a bit lost when we were all grounded, and bringing me into the Covid-19 WhatsApp fold (you all make me laugh every day and keep me connected to the flying world), but also for your humour and wisdom when I have confided in you about this book. I am also grateful that you pointed out that the original title sounded a bit like an advert for sanitary towels; hilarious as always, and completely to the point!

Heather, you may not realise how infectious your enthusiasm is for everything we have ever talked about. I hope that Dave would have been proud of this book, and it will forever be painful that he never got to read it. He was like another brother to me, and I hope I make him proud every day. Thank you for showing me what strength and dignity in the face of the ultimate loss looks like and for always being able to see the way forward.

There was a chain of events that started the book writing process and that began with Josh Winfield who contacted me initially to support Project Wingman and became a friend and mentor in so many ways during that time. It was Josh who originally said, "You should write a book," and then explained why. He sowed the seed, and I took it to an old university friend, Andrew Sharp. Thank you Andrew for loving the idea enough to connect me with Jason. It was Jason who told me to, "Just write everything down," which I did. It was then a conversation Jim had with his old schoolfriend Stephen Henley who reminded him that another friend, Oliver Wright, is a published author. Oliver, thank you for putting me in contact with Fisher King Publishing and introducing me to the wonder that is Rick Armstrong. Rick I can't thank you enough for seeing that my story had potential and choosing to not only take me on as an author but for all the encouragement you have given me along the way. I wouldn't have a book if it wasn't for you and that is something I will always be grateful for. Sam, thank you for your skilful editing of my original manuscript, I love the way you have done this without losing my voice, and also been so patient with me when you have needed me to send words through. Along with Rich and Rachel who have helped so much with marketing and putting together the book cover and so much more, I feel very lucky to be part of the Fisher King family. Thank you for making me so welcome.

An enormous part of this story, and the part that I believe my career was there to enable is Project Wingman, and that would never have happened without the help of an enormous number of people – 6,500 of them actually! I can't name them all of course, but if you volunteered for Wingman (and are therefore a Winglet), you are part of this story too, and I thank you from the bottom of my heart for being willing to stand up and be counted when it mattered the most, not only for our NHS friends, but for being there for each other and creating the most amazing community of aircrew friends.

There are some people I must thank personally. Esther Lisowski came on board after just three days when I was completely overwhelmed with the number of people who had signed up to help (750 in 72 hours). What you don't know about working a spreadsheet isn't worth knowing and I am so grateful to you for your friendship. We were destined to meet as instructors all those years ago, and Wingman is the reason.

The Wingman crew have not just been running a charity, but we have supported each other through all the highs and lows of the last four years. Zoe Ebrey for your wisdom and ability to explain in crayon! Lynsey Butcher for being wise counsel, always saying what needs to be said at just the right time, and knowing how to do things I can't even begin to imagine. Sarah Skelton for your unwavering support, kindness and sheer dedication to everything you take on. Carey Edwards for seeing the vision and helping to take it forward. Mark Flippence for driving things forward with such determination, and constantly badgering me to get back in the air. Ed Douglas for having such a wise head on such young shoulders and making sure we do things properly. Chris Carr because without you the buses would never go anywhere, ever. My right-hand man, Richard Griffin, not only do we have those buses because of you, but the sheer dedication you have given to Wingman since I promised you, that if you joined the board, it wouldn't be a heavy commitment, has been astonishing. I am sorry for all the hours you have ended up giving but I couldn't have done any of it without you, and for that you have my undying friendship; you literally can't get rid of me. Thank you all, for being part of what we have created.

There have been so many people along the way who have supported and cheered me on, and I am lucky to have had some strong mentors along that journey. Charlie Drew, thank you for all the crew room antics, answering the phone even though you know it's me and that I talk for hours, and for always being the tallest person in the room. George Hutton, you shaped a lot of my early career and were the only person who was prepared to be honest with me when I failed my command. I hope you know how valuable that was in making me a better captain the next time around. Also, thank you for always having a worse story than me when I was tearing my hair out with the stuff of children!

More recently, I have had the enormous pleasure of discovering a new career, as a professional speaker. Sarah Furness, thank you for supporting me and connecting me with Maria Franzoni who I adore and who has taught me how to become a professional speaker rather than someone who speaks. Mary Tillson-Wharton, thank you for helping me to know exactly what to say and how to deliver it. To all the other people in my new speaking community, including Mandy Hickson, Elliot Kay and Felicity Ashley, thank you for being part of the crew.

I know this is almost a chapter on its own, and also that there are so many people who have been important parts of the patchwork journey that has been my life so far; I have thanked so many, because there is a big difference between wanting to write a book, and actually writing it, and just in case I don't do it again, I wanted to put in black and white my thanks to as many as I can.

From the friends I made at university, and on Yorkshire Universities Air Squadron, at RAF Finningley, RAF Kinloss, Kinloss Rugby Club, RNZAF Whenuapai and the flying club there, Wycombe Air Park, Moray Flying Club and Inverness Airport. To all the easyJet crews I have had the joy of flying with. Moray Business Women, Surfable and the Stansted crew who still come and stay with me on Inverness nightstops. The Luton posse who have not only kept me sane but supported me along the way. The crew I have had the privilege of working with at Lyon and Porto, and finally at Gatwick where the dream unexpectedly came to an end. And now on to the next chapter with all the brilliant people I get to work with in a new world, I thank you all for your love and friendship, and for almost always saying yes when I ask if you can help with something!

The inspiration for everything I have ever tried to do has always been my family, who have shown me that no matter what happens, there is no problem that is too big to overcome, and no path you ever have to walk alone. Especially my Grandma. Grace by name and Grace by nature, it is her strength, resilience, faith in God and unwavering love and determination to keep calm and carry on right to the very end that has shaped and inspired me more than anyone else, so if there is a dedication to anyone, it must be to her, because without even realising it, she showed me what a strong woman looks like, and in her words, "I miss you dear."

Foreword

"Kia whakatōmuri te haere whakamua"
Trans: "I walk backwards into the future with my
eyes fixed on the past"
~ Maori Proverb

When I first started to fly, I just assumed that I would end up joining the RAF. It didn't occur to me then that the plans we make when we are young, rarely end up being anything like what actually happens during the course of our lives.

Similarly, when I returned to flying in my thirties, I assumed that I would stay working for easyJet until I retired having paid off the mortgage, got the children through school, university and maybe even weddings.

What should have been the end of my story couldn't have been further from everything that has happened since, and over the course of my adult life, my flying career, and my subsequent new career as a professional speaker and charity CEO, has been about making choices.

This is not the same thing as being in control all the time - although as a pilot, of course I am a complete control freak - what I mean is the choices I have made about how to manage things, where neccessary how to turn things on their heads, and how to learn and grow through them, because it is actually the failures and struggles in life that teach us the most about ourselves.

When I joined the University Air Squadron in 1993, women had only just been 'allowed' to start flying for the RAF again despite it being women who had ferried aircraft all around the country during the WWII, and those who did join had a tough path to carve for themselves in entering a man's world. I am grateful to all of those women, many of whom have gone on to be extremely successful in their chosen careers - and why wouldn't they be.

When I returned to flying after an eight year gap during which I had my children, built a house and moved to the other side of the world, it never occurred to me that there would be any barriers to me doing this - the support I had from my family, our friends at RNZAF Whenuapai, friends at home, former squadron mates and instructors was unequivocal, and there were only one or two occasions when I felt resentment from any of the men I worked with.

I was very lucky because it isn't like this for so many people, and when I was awarded the Diamond Jubilee Scholarship from the Guild of Air Pilots and Air Navigators to become an instructor, I vowed that I would always do what I could to support aspiring pilots, and promote the aviation industry wherever possible.

I have continued to do this, and some of my former flying students are now Captains at Cathay, BA and easyJet, and I still receive messages from people telling me that they were inspired to become a pilot by me, or that they are grateful for the support and encouragement I have been able to give them.

The key to all of this has been as simple as choosing to seek opportunities where challenges arise, and moving away from mistakes having learned how to do it differently the next time.

Our time living in New Zealand completely changed the course of our lives. When we went there, I wasn't sure what the point of it all was - we had just built our own house, decided to settle on the Moray Firth, and put our children into local schools rather than the military one on base. It didn't make sense, and yet it afforded us opportunities that were beyond our wildest dreams, and completely broadened our horizons. We became global citizens rather than the narrow minded, parochial people we had been before - and I think it is this different outlook on life that has allowed us as a family, and me personally, to push through the tougher part of life, and properly celebrate the wins.

Despite my children's protestations that the title of this book makes it sound as if I am either a coffee bean producer, or that I should be on the naughty step, it is deliberately chosen because when, in 2020 the world stopped, my career took a very unexpected turn. I was literally Grounded. My children are largely responsible for the fact that through everything that has happened since, I have been, and remain grounded as a person - I don't know any other way.

I hope this book provides the hope, inspiration and encouragement that is intended to everyone who reads it, that we are all capable of becoming the very best versions of ourselves we can be, and the message I want to shout from the rooftops is that the way we change the world is to make changes to the little corners of it that we inhabit. It really does make a difference.

When I had my children, I didn't ever plan or expect that they

would end up at boarding school so that I could pursue a career as a pilot. I can never know whether or not making a different decision would have been better - we made the decision with the knowledge we had at the time, and they have all grown into amazing adults. The one thing I can be sure of though is that I have shown my son and my daughters, and all of their friends, that women can pursue careers that are traditionally thought of as being male, and also be good mothers (or at least be the best mother possible). We can't however, have it all. There have been sacrifices along the way - but I hope I have shown my children that anything that is worth doing is worth working hard for.

The fact that there are still fewer than 500 female airline captains in the world today is part of the reason that I wanted to tell my story.

I have a voice, it is my responsibility to use it to benefit other people, I may be Grounded at the moment - but this isn't necessarily the end of my flying story - it never is when you fly - because flying is not something you do, flying is something you *are*.

Captain Emma Henderson MBE

Contents

Chapter One

Folding my Wings

It is 16th March 2020 and the last day in my working block before I start six days off. I begin the day in my own bed in my own house on the Moray Firth in the North of Scotland. Not a particularly remarkable thing for most people, but I spend a lot of my working life sleeping in someone else's house on the South Coast of England and I commute between the two. I am one of fewer than five hundred female airline pilots in the world - there are more endangered Bengal Tigers than that!

Over the last few years, I have reduced my working shifts to 75% so that I can spend more time at home, and as a result, life is good. This means that instead of working what is known as a 5453 pattern where you work 5 days, have 4 days off, then work 5 days and have 3 off, before starting the pattern again, I work a 465346 pattern, 4 on, 6 off, 5 on and so forth. I have also managed to bid for as many Inverness night stops as possible; I work for an airline that usually returns to base every night, with three exceptions from London Gatwick where I have worked for the last two and a half years. These are Madrid, Milan and Inverness! So, this is how I get to wake up in my own house on 16th March and spend the morning at home before driving to the airport to check in with my crew who have spent the night in a local hotel, to operate to Gatwick, and then on to Luxembourg and back.

The year so far feels like it is full of promise and although I have always loved flying, really loved flying an airliner full of people, and especially love being the captain, the last few months have been fun as well. Aircrew, the mix of pilots and cabin crew or flight attendants, are almost always attached to a 'base' unless they inhabit the hallowed space known as the Private Jet world where they will instead have a 'gateway' meaning they report for duty at their local airport to be transported to wherever in the world they are needed. The likes of us lowly airline pilots, however, have bases to which we must live close enough to be called from a standby duty and, within ninety minutes, arrive ready for work and smartly turned out with a spring in our steps within ninety minutes.

For the first five years of my career my base was London Stansted airport, after which I moved to Luton which was much closer to anywhere my RAF husband was ever going to be posted, and therefore made more sense. Having demanded that we return home to the Moray Firth in 2018, I then moved to Gatwick on the basis that you should always be based at the place where you can most easily commute to (you might be surprised at the number of pilots who commute not only up and down the country but also to and from Europe on a regular basis) and within a few weeks I had been asked to appear in a documentary being made by ITV called 'easyJet, Inside the Cockpit'. The first series had not been well received and the second series aimed to show the human side of what it's like to have one of the coolest offices in the world. After meeting with the production team, I agreed, on the basis that it must be done in a way which highlights the profession rather than causes embarrassment.

For the last few weeks, the news has been dominated by a new virus that has reportedly been spreading from China. No one really knows what to make of it but there is a lot of uncertainty and plenty of talk of aircraft being grounded and travel stopping in order to stop the spread. We have been constantly reassured by our airline management that there is nothing to worry about, measures are in place to keep us all safe and scientific guidance is being followed; for now, everyone is still flying as usual.

Before leaving for work, I have walked the dogs on the beach, a cold jaunt but so good for the soul - one of the reasons we settled here in the first place is the miles and miles of long, sandy, and often empty beaches backed with pine forests which provide great shelter on the days when it's so windy you end up being sandblasted if you try your luck in the open. Sometimes there are really fierce winds to contend with flying in and out of Inverness, and at the other extreme, very occasionally, the sea mist, known locally as the Haar, rolls in and everything grinds to a halt. We can take off in this weather, but we can't land. Today though, the weather is nothing special, and as I so often do, I use the drive to work to think about the day ahead and try to remember if I have actually been to Luxembourg before, I think I may have done years ago as a First Officer, but this will be the first time I have been since I got my command four years ago. My crew is always lovely, but today I am flying with people who have become friends - it's going to be a good day.

I park at the Flying Club at the far end of the airport and make the short walk into the terminal, passing passengers as I go who will be on my flight in just over an hour, and greet my crew. They have had a pleasant morning, and we are all looking forward to getting on with the job we are there to do. Our aircraft is on final approach coming in from Gatwick as we all troop through the single arch that makes up crew security and my First Officer and I check the Flight Plans we have been handed, make our fuel decisions, and brief the crew. There is not too much to discuss about today and as we take over the aircraft from the inbound crew, talk turns again to the 'virus' that seems to be more of a concern as each day goes by.

Both pilots on a commercial airliner are equally qualified to operate the aircraft and so we take it in turns to be the 'pilot flying' on each flight which is known as a 'sector'. The difference between the two pilots is usually one of experience; it is not always the case, but the captain is usually much more experienced than the right-hand seat pilot (the First Officer) and often, I am also much older. However, age and gender are irrelevant in a flight deck, we are both simply pilots and we have already decided that I will operate the flight to Gatwick, the First Officer will fly to Luxembourg, and I will fly back to Gatwick. The previous day, we operated to Edinburgh and back before making the trip to Inverness to night stop. The First Officer operated the first two flights on that day with me bringing the aircraft into Inverness - wherever possible we try and spread the routes between us.

As Pilot Flying, it is my job to perform a walk around to visually inspect the aircraft - the pilot's version of 'kicking the tyres' - we check everything we can see or touch and also sign for the fuel that has been loaded for our flight to Gatwick. Once back on board, I programme the flight plan into the onboard computer, we both run through performance calculations on separate purpose-built onboard tablets, and we brief the expected taxi routing and take off. Meanwhile our passengers are boarding and as has become my habit over the last four years, I go into the cabin to welcome everyone on board from the front, saying hello to one or two familiar faces as I go - I operate this flight a lot and also live locally so it is not unusual at all to see people I know amongst the passengers.

I love flying into and out of Inverness. It is so spectacular even on a seemingly grey day and I can often see as far as where my house is as we come in on our final approach. On departure though, we take off facing to south west and very quickly we have climbed high above Inverness itself and are making our way south over the Cairngorms, past Edinburgh and Glasgow and back into the airspace that is controlled by London rather than Scottish air traffic control.

The day runs to plan. The flights are short, and we have to make sure we have programmed, checked and briefed our arrival into each destination as well as finding time to eat. There is still time however, to talk, and Coronavirus or Covid-19 is rapidly dominating everything in the news and our conversation. Rumours are flying around and in parts of Europe including Italy, things are already presented as being really bad. Two days before

I had managed to grab a rare opportunity to spend time with my brothers-in-law in London and when I had arrived at theirs, one of them was not feeling great so opted to stay well clear of me, and everyone else just in case it was something more sinister than a cold. I had a lovely evening with my husband's brother and our nephews and was also able to spend the next morning with them before heading off to work. By the time I arrived at Gatwick, I had a message to say that my brother-in-law had deteriorated, had tested positive for Covid and was isolating. He is asthmatic so it was really worrying and ultimately, it took him over two weeks to recover. Having received this information, I didn't know where I stood in terms of being safe to fly. I had just arrived at work so took advice from my base management team who were happy that this posed no risk, and I could continue with my duties. This was early days and the information we had about the virus was still limited and none of us can do anything other than work with the data we have in front of us at the time. I was still permitted to fly and so off I went. This was something we discussed during our flights on our way down from Inverness and out to Luxembourg and back, and because we had boarded the flight in Inverness, and not entered the terminal that day, none of us really even realised how suddenly the bustling terminals at Gatwick had emptied and become ghost towns.

It doesn't take long to get to Luxembourg from Gatwick, in fact my logbook tells me that the flight each way was a little over an hour and although the numbers were down, we were blessed with lovely passengers and it was a clear and calm night as we made our way back to London, with fantastic views over northern France, the Channel, and the South of England.

There was, however, something else in the air that night which made us feel that the flight we had just operated was somehow significant. Whether it was anticipation of our impending doom or just a realisation that a tidal wave was rushing towards us and we were trapped on the beach, unable to escape its inevitability, I will never know, but ultimately, although I did not know it at the time, this was a very significant flight for me because it turned out to be the last flight in eleven years at my airline, in a career that has spanned thirty years, and covered five different bases, and four decades of my life.

We all felt quite sad saying goodbye to the few passengers we brought back from Luxembourg, and they all wish us luck as they left which is not something we would normally hear; we all felt as if something big was about to happen. The mood was lightened considerably when one of the crew, a lovely and true gentleman named Peter, found a green rubber ball shaped child's squeezy toy with bits sticking out of it and he came rushing forward saying, "I've found the virus! I have it here! Quick let's get rid of it and save the world!" We all fell about laughing and then got on with closing the aircraft down for the night.

Once an aircraft is parked on stand, there are two ways it can be powered. One way is by using a small engine at the very back of the aircraft called an Auxiliary Power Unit or APU. This is switched on during the taxi in from the runway so that a constant supply of power is available to the aircraft, it also enables us to shut down one of the engines as only one is required for taxiing which saves fuel. Once on stand, with both the main engines shut down, more often than not, a lead is plugged into the aircraft by the ground crew, and this provides electrical power instead so the APU can be shut down. On leaving the aircraft there are a number of checks that need to be conducted by the flight crew with the final thing being to switch off the batteries, having made sure the ground power can still be accessed by the cleaners when they come on board during the night. Everything goes dark and quiet after the noise of the operating day, and it's a moment of stillness we all enjoy. I confess that I felt quite deflated that night as I closed the aircraft door and walked down the steps for what would turn out to be the final time.

As I walked away from the aircraft that night, as I always did, I looked back to check it was all ok. I felt like I was saying goodbye to a dear friend. This might sound silly and sentimental, but during my eleven years working for an airline, I have spent an entire year in the flight deck of an Airbus A319 or A320 and it was a familiar and safe environment that I knew my way around. I loved everything about it from the big wide windows meaning that every day I flew I saw bright sunshine, to the side stick we use to fly, as opposed to the yoke of most small aircraft or a Boeing passenger jet, the genius of the much coveted tray table that pulled out from beneath my two instrument screens, and the general sense of space there was in what was otherwise a little room at the front of an aircraft where all the magic supposedly happens. I also loved knowing that there were hundreds of onboard computers processing information, and making things happen, and the vast panel of buttons and switches above our heads that were laid out in what seemed to me to be a logical order and were just a normal part of my working day. This space had safely transported me and my passengers to hundreds of destinations across the UK, Europe and North Africa over more than a decade, and represented a lot of hard work but also a lot of fun, so walking away from that aircraft, on that night in March 2020 was just like walking away from an old pal and not knowing when you would see them again.

Having spent the night in my digs on the south coast, the next day, I drove on empty roads back to an empty Gatwick, parked in an empty car park, walked to the terminal and caught an empty shuttle to the South Terminal to catch an empty train straight through London to Luton, took an empty bus up to that Terminal which was also silent and still and quite eerie. I had been based at Luton for almost four years and I don't think there was ever a time when I walked through the terminal on duty or as a passenger, when it wasn't completely heaving with people. Seeing what I knew to be such a busy place, empty and quiet was something I never thought I would experience - and it was extremely uncomfortable. My flight to Inverness was unusually early - that particular flight always came in from an early rotation to Paris Charles de Gaulle and often ran a little behind - to be early was very unusual but what was even more uncommon was that it too was almost empty.

The flight is something that is so familiar to me, I have operated it hundreds of times and travelled on it as a passenger almost as many, not to mention all the time I spent flying 'bugsmashers' around the local area teaching people how to fly in my past life as an instructor. Inverness is uncomplicated - although there is a published instrument approach plate, most of the time you point at the airfield and get taken off on an easterly heading descending along the beautiful Moray coast past Nairn and out along the sand edged forests of Culbin (famous for being the home of Macbeth's three witches) and then turning to the north to start what is called the 'base turn', but not before I have had a glimpse of home. Findhorn bay stretching out before me, with the now closed runway of Kinloss - another place where I spent so much time teaching people to fly - and if I look just to the right, I can see the space where I know my house is, just briefly before we make the turn back in towards the south westerly runway, bringing back the speed, lowering flaps and landing gear before we reach the 1000 foot cut off point, and bringing 60 odd tonnes of metal gracefully down on the tarmac once more. At least that's the idea and it was a matter of personal pride that the landing and especially the braking at Inverness particularly should be smooth. It is more important to land on the correct part of the runway than how smooth the landing is, but something of a bugbear to me was always the braking.

Pilots have performance software at their disposal which must be used before every landing to confirm that the conditions at the airfield and weight and status of the aircraft will allow a safe landing. This becomes more critical when a runway is considered to be short as is the case at Inverness. Landing on a 4000m runway isn't going to cause anyone too many headaches, but when the landing distance is only 1800m, you need to know you can do it - which almost all of the time we can. The exceptions would be if something had failed on the aircraft (something that happens so infrequently on modern passenger jets that the only time we get to experience it is in twice yearly simulator checks we must all do), or much more frequently, if the wind is too strong and from the wrong direction such as across the runway.

However most of the time, landing at Inverness is the same as landing anywhere else but there is a perception amongst pilots that because the runway is shorter than some we fly into, the maximum amount of braking must be used as soon as the aircraft touches down - the wheels slam onto the runway and you are thrown forward in your seat as the aircrafts automatic braking system (selected to MEDIUM rather than LOW) kicks in. It's not necessary as there is plenty of room to land, use the lower brake setting and bring the aircraft to a safe taxi speed well before the end of the runway. I always used to silently roll my eyes when travelling as a passenger and a lovely landing was ruined by the inevitable lurch forward of all the passengers as the aircraft slowed from its touchdown speed of 120Mph to around 25mph which is the fastest speed at which we may taxi - and of course this was always so much more fun when travelling in uniform and I could feel the eyes of the passengers around me looking to see whether or not I approved of the landing. Obviously, it all came down in the end to whether or not the captain was a friend of mine or not - if they were, I would do my best to look impressed, if they were either unknown, or, on a rare occasion, unpleasant, they would definitely get an eye roll!

Being based at Gatwick, for me, landing in Inverness always meant getting off and going home while the rest of the crew spent a night in a hotel in the city, and it was always a good feeling to be signing the aircraft logbook to confirm all the details of the completed flight knowing that I would be walking out to my car to drive home and spend the night in my own bed. Today though, it was not my aircraft, and I had no idea that I would never travel on an easyJet aircraft again as one of its employees.

As was usually the case, I knew the Luton based crew and before I left we all chatted and said our goodbyes, wished each other luck, and I drove home for my days off.

During that time at home, rumours of a full lockdown started to spread, and I was rostered on one flight to Italy that I was really reluctant to operate for two reasons - firstly the news coming out of Italy itself screamed DO NOT COME HERE to me even though we were still flying there, and secondly, I didn't want to get stuck in England. I called my boss and asked her for advice - she told me not to come down as there were local pilots who would be more than happy to operate the flight on my behalf. The flight never happened, and it was a good job that I stayed at home as we went into lockdown, all flights were grounded, and I may not have been able to return home for two months.

My car remained in the staff car park at Gatwick until a friend could collect it and store it on her driveway, and I sat at home wondering what would come next - which as it turns out, was another of the big challenges that have made up the patchwork quilt of my life! You see, rather than sit at home enjoying the astonishingly brilliant weather we had that spring and summer, I founded a charity called Project Wingman, which I am still running today.

Chapter 2

In the Beginning

RAF Finningley, October 1993

"Can we stop the bus please?" The driver looks bemused and given that we are currently doing 70mph on a motorway somewhere between Doncaster and Leeds, I don't blame him. "Actually, we really need to stop the bus," the voice is more urgent now - there are twelve of us all dressed smartly in suits, and ranging from 'slightly pissed' to 'steaming' on the piss-ometer scale. I am actually quite relieved when, having presumably weighed up the risk vs benefit of stopping on the side of a motorway to let people relieve themselves, or carrying on and some of them doing it anyway, the driver pulls on to the hard shoulder and the boys all pile out. I realise that I also can't wait until we are deposited back at the University building and so I jump out and join them, much to the admiration of my soon to be colleagues.

Bugger! I am looking in disbelief at my own stupidity, as a RAF Medical Officer waits for the answer to what should be a really simple question, but which I have managed to spectacularly screw up, "...and do you have your glasses with you?"

It is a simple question, and the answer should be, "Yes of course, I will put them on so that I can complete this eye test and pass my aircrew medical." I am stubborn about my glasses though. I hate wearing them. I always have, ever since the first pair of clear white plastic framed NHS glasses were handed to me when I was in junior school. They may have stopped me from getting piercing headaches caused by desperately squinting at the blackboard in my 1970s classroom, but they were hideous and by the time I am at University I have stopped wearing them altogether. That is until I realise that I can't see the screens in lectures and I force myself to go and take another eye test, this time choosing a highly fashionable pair of specs which I only wear when I have to - even they were hideous given that it is the 1990s and almost no fashion sense had arrived in the world of eyewear.

I am interviewing for a place on the Yorkshire Universities Air Squadron, only the second intake that has included girls - somehow, despite the vast numbers of women who flew during WWII, fifty years later, the RAF, in 1993 is not only still dominated by men but only just starting to accept the idea that girls can fly too. I want a place on this squadron so badly and I have spent weeks making sure I am up to date on current affairs, I now own a suit to make sure I am dressed appropriately, and I have thought long and hard about what my answer will be if I am asked about my thoughts on whether or not I would be prepared to drop bombs in the event of a war. I have even made sure I know as much as I can find out in those pre-internet days about what the RAF actually does - I don't come from a military family so this is not as easy as it would be today when each University Air Squadron probably has its own Tik Tok account.

Despite all this careful preparation however, I have still

managed to overlook one, admittedly, fairly important thing. I will need to have perfect vision to be able to fly, and since I don't, I will need to prove that my vision can be corrected enough by passing an eye test wearing my glasses. The glasses that were currently sitting on my desk in the gloomy, glossy brown painted room with the dodgy gas fire that is my student digs. Not much use there!

Much to my surprise this is not the problem I think it will be. We do all the eye tests anyway, confirm that I am indeed short sighted, and then move on to the Isihara plates - you know those circles of coloured dots that are supposed to have numbers in them. I am completely stumped. "What do you see in this circle?" I stare moronically at the circle of coloured splodges, desperately willing something to appear to me as if I can somehow magic an answer. Nothing. All I can see is circles of colour. "And how about this one?" Again, nothing. This process is repeated and I am starting to think it's some kind of trick - maybe the SMO is testing me to make sure I don't see things that are not there... I am clutching at straws but this is insane, there is NOTHING in the circles. The SMO makes some notes, "I would like to refer you to one of our eye specialists," he says, "have you ever been told you are colour-blind before?" I haven't, but that explains a lot about why I always wear strangely matched clothes!

My heart sinks as I brace myself to be told that due to my eyesight I will not make the selection but this doesn't happen and after the interviews we all gather in the Squadron bar for introductory drinks with some of the current squadron members and instructors - actually a lot of introductory drinks including the memorably named 'Tigers Wank' - so called because it is a mixture of Advocat and Black Sambuca which separates to make a yellow and black drink, matching the squadron colours.

It is therefore not really surprising that we need to pull over on to the hard shoulder for a pee on the way home, and I have never been able to remember how it is that having been deposited at the front of the University building in Leeds, I manage to navigate my way across the notorious Hyde Park, back into the student ghetto of Headingley and home. I wake up the next morning lying on my bed, still in my suit and feeling like I have just been hit by a train. Welcome to the Yorkshire Universities Air Squadron!

"OK Emma, I am just going to hop out and stretch my legs, so if you would like to go and do that again by yourself, I will see you back here in about ten minutes and you can pick me up and we will taxi back to the squadron together shall we."

I am about to burst with a mixture of pride, excitement and a healthy dose of fear. My squadron boss has just cleared me for my first solo flight after just a few hours of instruction. I am the first of my intake to do this and I pinch myself to make sure it is real. "Right then sir, thank you very much, see you shortly," I reply and he clambers out of our Bulldog training aircraft XX690 and smiles, "don't forget to enjoy it!" He secures his harness and I close the canopy, waiting until he is clear before I run through my drills. Check for full and free movement of the flight controls, check the temperature and pressure gauges with the engine running at 50% power, held against the brakes, check the mixture is correct, and then I am speaking to Air Traffic Control asking for permission to taxi to the runway for one solo circuit.

"XX690 Runway Two Zero Cleared Take Off Wind Two One Zero Five Knots," I hear over my headset and I read this back before pushing the throttle forward, releasing the brakes and feeling the aircraft move slowly at first, then gathering speed until at only 65 knots, I am airborne. On my own. For the first time in my life and all I can do is focus on making sure I do everything I am supposed to do. Set the pitch to get the correct climb angle, retract the flaps that were used for take off (they will come out again for landing but I don't need them in the meantime), make sure I don't bust my circuit altitude, watch as the long runway of RAF Finningley disappears below me and I level off at 1000 feet above the ground, looking for the visual references I will use to fly my circuit. I can see the power stations of South Yorkshire with their little puffs of smoke at the top of their enormous cooling towers, and now I am downwind, flying parallel to the runway, I have checks I must perform - I run through these from memory, like all the checks I have had to learn, speaking to Air Traffic Control as I go. "XX690 Downwind Two Zero Full Stop," tells them that I will be landing from this approach and vacating the runway.

For a few brief moments, I am suspended in the air, having completed my checks and knowing what I need to do next, and I look out of the large perspex canopy completely thrilled at what is happening. This is where I want to be. I complete the circuit, selecting flaps in stages to allow the little aircraft to slow down, receive my landing clearance and touch down on the runway again, slowing down as I reach the exit where my boss is waiting for me with a beaming face. I am handed over to the Ground Frequency by the Tower, "Contact Ground 121.625 and Congratulations on your first solo flight Ma'am." We will be celebrating in the bar tonight that's for sure!

"There is a little wiggle in the lake to the west of Diss, do you see that it points straight at Honington, so if you follow that, it will bring you straight back here." One of the older squadron members Nathan is dispensing this wise advice and I listen in - I am about to fly my Solo Sector Recce as it is called - a navigation exercise that if flown well enough with an instructor, will then be flown alone. It is four months since my first solo flight and I have another 25 hours of flying time to my name. We are nearing the end of a two week Summer Camp at RAF Honington in Suffolk, two weeks of idyllic East Anglian summer weather, with barely a cloud in the sky, and plenty of flying to be had including one day when someone's dad flies his Chinook in to visit us and we are all given a ride over Constable Country with the doors open - something I find exhilarating and terrifying in equal measure - I have still never really taken to helicopters!

This is familiar territory for me having grown up a bit further south in the Essex countryside. I have cousins nearby and Diss is a town I know. I study the map and see that there is indeed a 'wiggle in the lake' that points directly back to Honington. 'Well that makes life simple,' I think to myself, 'I shall just follow that and find my way home.'

It turns out that there are two 'wiggles' in the lake to the west of Diss. One points to RAF Honington and the other one - well, doesn't. I realise, after pointing in what I think is the right direction, that I should be back at Honington by now, and all I can see is the flat countryside stretching for miles in front of me. I can't even see Diss behind me any more. I can feel my heart pounding in my chest as I think about what I should do. I have a map with my route carefully plotted out on it, but it is almost useless now as I clearly haven't been following it anyway. 'Why did you listen to stupid Nathan and not just follow the tracks you marked on your map you dimwit,' I silently scream at myself. I feel sweat forming on my face behind my visor and my bone dome with its built in headset suddenly feels very heavy. I can see the headlines, 'Trainee pilot lands in muddy field due to extreme and unavoidable stupidity.' I am in radio contact with my instructor in the old Air Traffic Control Tower at Honington and I realise that I have to bite the bullet and confess. "XX709 err request grid reference." There is silence and I later find out that my instructor and everyone else who can hear the radios are actually wetting themselves laughing in the moments it takes for them to process that I have managed to get myself lost. "A grid reference? Are you lost," is the reply. I can't admit defeat completely, "No sir, not lost, just temporarily unaware of my position," apparently this too is met with howls of laughter. "Are you over some woods?' I am actually getting a bit worried now. 'Of course I'm over some woods, I'm in Norfolk - I think.' I decide to orbit to see if I can see any landmarks at all and within what feels like several hours but is in fact only a couple of minutes, my instructor is back on the radio giving me a steer back to Honington which is actually not too far away. I land with more than a small feeling of relief and as I taxi back to the squadron building, I wonder what the fire engine is there for - it is not unknown for people who do stupid things to be hosed down by the fire crew and I realise that this must be my fate. "Thank goodness it is summer," I mutter as I shut down the engine, secure the aircraft and remove my bone dome, my hair is damp from the sweat and the slight breeze feels delicious and cool after the heat of the situation and being inside the canopy. I brace myself as I walk back to the building, ready to throw my helmet out of the way if it looks like it will get wet, but the fire engine is not for me, well not directly anyway. The full story unravels during my debrief and will be the source of gentle ribbing for years to come - thoroughly deserved, of course.

Having followed the wrong 'wiggle' I had not only flown off course, but actually entered the protected airspace around the large US Air Force base of Lakenheath, not far from Honington. Word quickly spread that there was a solo student pilot bimbling around somewhere inside their Military Air Traffic Zone, or MATZ as it is known, completely lost, and until I was found, all movements were suspended. As I am told of this the weight of my error comes crashing down onto my shoulders, but there is more. In order to find me, the radar has been switched on in the old ATC building. I am found and returned to base, but in the meantime, the radar has overheated and since there is no longer air conditioning to keep it cool, it began to smoulder. Whether or not there were any actual flames I didn't dare ask and don't want to know, but when it is time for me to leave the squadron, the traditional Squadron Print, in this case a picture of the Bulldog I have been flying, is covered in comments from instructors and colleagues alike, 'keep an eye on the woods,' 'keep asking for grid references,' and, 'are you lost?'

I am duly 'fined' for my stupidity on a Pigs board we keep in the bar; each square is worth a fiver and my bill is hefty, but not as hefty as it could have been, and I take it on the chin. This was my mistake alone, and I learned two things, firstly the importance of owning your mistakes and not blaming others, and secondly, and perhaps most importantly, I am not cut out to be a navigator!

Chapter Three

Unforecast Turbulence

It is December 2013 and I am on a line check from my base in Stansted to Prague and back with a Training Captain called Dave Gauntlett in the jump seat; the jump seat is a third seat in the flight deck intended for exactly this purpose, to allow a training captain to carry out a check of your operational capability during a normal flight from A to B and back. It is usual that in the winter, you end up flying more in the darkness than you do in the daylight, and today is no exception. At some point during the flight, I comment that I am tired to which Dave replied, "Emma, you are always tired these days. I think your commute is not good for you, it can't be easy living as far away as you do."

I am instantly defensive. My husband is a RAF officer, and we live in MOD accommodation in the small village of Halton in Buckinghamshire. My drive to work is long but straightforward, and crucially, within the magic ninety minutes required by my company. Straight down the A41 to the M25, then on to the M11 and off at the Stansted exit. At the times of day, I travel to and from work it takes eighty minutes to drive the sixty miles to work because it is all on the motorway. If I really need it, I have the bolthole of being able to stay with my parents in the house in which I grew up which is only thirty minutes away (but in the wrong direction).

I have spent my entire career juggling my commute to work

with where we need to live because of my husband's job and I don't think anything of this drive, downloading books on Audible to break up the monotony of the journey, sometimes catching up on phone calls (hands free of course) and fairly regularly listening to the shipping forecast, gauging how long my day had been on occasions by catching the morning and the evening broadcast during the drive. I should add that I love the shipping forecast. It is still magical to me and one of my favourite books is by Charlie Connelly, Attention all Shipping, which describes his journey around all the points on the shipping forecast!

I grew up in Essex and spent a large amount of my teenage years sailing dinghies on the River Blackwater with a Charitable Trust called Fellowship Afloat that my parents had been involved with right from when I was a baby; I was six weeks old when I was first taken onto a boat. Obviously, I do not remember this momentous occasion but spent a lot of time in the small village of Tollesbury where the Trust is still based, initially learning to sail and then spending my summers as a volunteer sailing instructor and galley assistant preparing meals for groups of up to sixty people. At first, this was on an old Thames Sailing Barge called Memory, and then, after Memory tragically burned out one cold winter, on a decommissioned light vessel appropriately called Trinity as the Trust was and still is a Christian organisation. They were halcyon days, spending all our time outside regardless of the weather although I always remember it as being hot and sunny. One of our tasks in the morning was to listen to the shipping forecast to find out what we could expect during the days sailing. Remember this was in the late 1980s and early 1990s and only people like my dad who is a businessman had 'mobile' phones (the size of house bricks). You had to be able to write really fast and be ready when the time came because it wasn't repeated and there was no way of rewinding. I am certain that those days of needing information from the shipping forecast were what founded my love of listening to it on my commute to and from work - it is connected with happy memories of carefree days.

My working pattern means that for five days I make this journey to Stansted before having three or four days off with one block of five days being early starts and the next block being late finishes. It is how things work at my airline and allows for some degree of planning, although I am very aware of the toll that waking up at 0330 one week to arrive home at 0200 the following week is not good for me or anyone else for that matter; circadian rhythm is not something any of us should be messing with.

I have always been blessed with good health and a strong constitution and have taken pride over the last four years of airline flying that I have never had a day off sick, but lately I have been experiencing the sort of symptoms that a lot of airline pilots seem to suffer with; similar to IBS but not as bad, but gastro type symptoms which make life uncomfortable rather than unbearable. Like most people in aviation, I ignore them and put it down to bad diet, lack of sleep, alcohol, on the rare occasions I drink - when you work shifts there are not many times when you can drink and anyway, I need to get good quality sleep rather than to be in an alcohol induced coma. The symptoms are mild and sporadic, but

I have noticed that I am getting more tired.

By the spring of 2014 I know there is something wrong, but I can't put my finger on it. I have no visible symptoms, I am just exhausted on my days off, and I have a kind of aching feeling in the top of my back that feels like a deep muscle fatigue. I am fit and strong and otherwise healthy, and I run and play tennis every day even when I am working, as well as regularly swimming, banging out 1,000m without even thinking about it - there can't be anything seriously wrong with me if I can do all of that, right?

Maybe it's a vitamin deficiency. I up my game with making sure I am eating healthily, and I have never looked or felt as fit as I do during that spring, but there is still something wrong. The doctor decides to run blood tests and on the back of those results, and my explanation of how I am feeling, he books me in for a scan at Stoke Mandeville hospital which is almost next door.

The night before the scan, we have an overnight visit from one of our closest friends Baz, who is also in the RAF and is working at High Wycombe for a couple of days. We have known Baz and his wife Jane since our early days at RAF Finningley when my husband was going through his Navigator Training, and I was a cadet pilot on the finest University Air Squadron in the country – Yorkshire, obviously. We all ended up together at RAF Kinloss, had our children together and have carried each other through the highs and lows that life brings, and something of a tradition is that when Baz comes to stay, my husband always falls asleep around 11pm and Baz and I stay up and put the world to rights until way into the small hours of the morning. We are heroes, until the alarm goes off and we realise we are no longer in our early twenties.

This night is no exception and being one of the rarer occasions when I do drink, I have the mother of all hangovers the next morning which feels like it is starting to subside a little by the time I have to go to the hospital later on in the afternoon. Little is said during the scan, and I am duly sent back to the doctor for the results. I am relieved to be told that everything was normal but shocked that the reason for the scan was to rule out ovarian cancer.

In the meantime, my hangover doesn't seem to want to clear up and develops into the kind of flu that makes you realise that you have never had the flu before. I am really sick. I can't get out of bed and on the occasions I make it downstairs it takes a long time to climb them again. I am completely floored. Like everyone else, I can take a week off work by 'self-certifying' and as long as I fill in a form to explain my absence no questions are asked. As a future base captain would tell me, "We trust you to fly a $100M aircraft around Europe, we therefore trust you to know when you can't." But after a week I am no better and I end up having to get antibiotics and a sick note from the doctor. All in all, I have been off work for almost a month by the time I return which I am not happy about, anyone who flies will understand this, when you fly, it's almost like you need to fly, in the same way as running becomes addictive I suppose flying does too. Having been up there where the air is rarified, as Frank Sinatra would sing, a little bit of your heart will always remain. I am desperate to get back to work and to get my hands back on my beloved Airbus A319. My licence allows me to operate the A319, A320 and A321, but at Stansted we mostly have the smaller A319s which carry 156 passengers and you can land them on a fence as they say - I love them and I have missed seeing my flying friends while I have been away.

By now it is May and although I have recovered, there is still something that doesn't feel right. I am back running, playing tennis and swimming, and have entered some races to give me something to work towards. Every week on a Tuesday night, I meet a group of other ladies from the tennis club, and we go for a run around the surrounding villages; it is always a laugh because we gossip while we run. On one of these Tuesdays, I struggle, and I assume it is because I am still building up fitness from being sick, but the following Saturday at Tennis, I fall over. I tend to clown around a bit when playing tennis. I am not a terrible player, but I will never set the tennis world on fire and have no desire to do so, I just get maximum enjoyment out of everything I do, so when I fall over, we all laugh, I get up, we continue. A week later the same thing happens, and again the following Thursday at which point a lovely friend, Andrea, says, "You know what mate, that's the third time you have fallen over recently, are you sure everything is alright?" I reply that I am fine, just clumsy and a bit of a wally, but something needles at me. I don't know if I am OK.

The following Tuesday, I collapse during a run. One minute I was running, the next minute my legs won't move at all. I manage to get back on my feet and walk the rest of the way, but it is definitely time to see a doctor.

There is nothing anyone can hang their hats on with what is happening to me and blood tests are all normal apart from one thing, which is that my Vitamin D levels are very low, most people in the UK are vitamin D deficient but I am a complete sun worshipper, outside all the time and not in any way ashamed to spend a lot of time in a bikini in my hammock - everyone who knows me understands that this is my main pastime and I am therefore tanned as if I have just spent a month in the Mediterranean - my vitamin D levels should not be low. The tests are repeated just in case and the levels are even lower. This is the only clue the doctor has and I am still as active as I always have been, just sleeping more.

On 25th May, I travel to London with my tennis club running friends to take part in the BUPA London 10k which I have been training for despite the occasional tumble. I need to finish the race and then get home in time to get to work as I am operating the late Malaga from Stansted that evening. It is a glorious May Day and London has never looked so lovely as we all gather in St James's Park for the start of the race. We edge our way down the Mall after Mo Farah has fired the starters pistol for all the hot shots and professionals at the front of the enormous crowd, laughing and chatting as we are looking forward to this iconic run. And then it's time for us to get going. Running down the Mall we start to separate, and I run with Isla, as is often the case - we are both a little slower than the others and we are quite happy for them to head off and do their own thing. Turning right on to Whitehall it happens again, my legs give way and I somehow manage to stop myself from falling, but I am frightened, and now I am holding Isla up. She offers to run with me, but I wave her on saying I will just slow her down. I am determined to finish this race, and I do. It is a fantastic route along the Embankment to Blackfriars, up towards St Pauls and then into the city as I know it, familiar from years of idolising my dad's world of Lloyds and the square mile of iconic buildings that makes up the City of London. I will never forget running through Leadenhall Market which is completely empty apart from us runners and the sound of our trainers is pretty much all I could hear. It is brilliant but slow, it takes me an agonising one hour and twenty minutes to complete what should have taken me fifty minutes but I have done it and I am so relieved to turn the corner from Birdcage Walk back towards the Palace where I meet up with my friends, collect my medal, bat off concerns about whether or not I am fit and well, take the train home and go to work.

That was to be the last race I ran for a very long time, but I didn't know it then.

As the days pass the dull ache that had begun in my back is also becoming noticeable in my right arm and I just can't seem to shake the low level but constant feeling that I need to stretch. I have another appointment scheduled with the doctor in the afternoon of the 18th of June after I have operated an early Copenhagen. I am finished work by one thousand and in the crew room I bump into one of my closest friends, Graham, from my type rating training; airline pilots have to go through a specific training course for each aircraft type they fly - in this case it was the Airbus Type Rating course. Four of us from the course had ended up at Stansted and Graham is one of those rare people who can make you laugh just by looking at you, in fact he had done this with devastating effect twice during the course, and on one occasion, I had to leave the room and pretend I needed the loo just so I could compose myself. It is always lovely to bump into Graham and we stand chatting as I check out and he checks in for his flights for the day. Typically, I drop my pen while we are talking, crouch down to pick it up, to the usual banter that goes backwards and forwards between us, and then realise I can't stand up. "Graham can you pull me up please?" I ask. He looks at me and giggles thinking I am messing around. "No, Graham can you actually pull me up please." He must have seen the panicked look in my eyes, his face changes completely as he pulls me up to standing and I quickly explain what has been going on and that I am seeing the doctor later that day. "Shit," is the most appropriate response I think I ever got from anyone - there is really nothing else to say.

I see the doctor that afternoon and she wants to refer me to a neurologist as she wants to rule out potential issues. I have never been one for pussy footing around, so I just ask her directly if she thinks I have Multiple Sclerosis. Her reply that she wants to rule it out feels to me like doctor speak for, 'yes but I don't want to scare you.' I brace myself for what the future might look like.

It is a really hot day and when I get home I decide I need the hammock more than ever before as I now need to phone my Aviation Medical Examiner (AME) and tell him what's happening; every commercial pilot must hold a Class One Medical issued by the Civil Aviation Authority and there is an obligation on the part of the pilot to inform them of any potential medical downgrade. He is reassuring, calm and takes me through what needs to happen next which is that I need to see him the following day and that my medical will be suspended pending investigation until we know more. The next phone call is to my base Captain George. George is something of a legend at Stansted and I have always had a really good relationship with him. Starting at Stansted in early 2010, his advice to the four of us was, "Work hard, keep your head down, keep your nose clean and you'll be right." I like George, he is straight talking, and I believe he genuinely has people's best interests at heart, he is also a Kiwi, and we have plenty to talk about having lived in New Zealand for over three years on a diplomatic posting and with a brother who has lived there since he was twenty. I arrange to visit George the next afternoon.

I feel a bit fraudulent as I drive to Stansted the next day to meet Peter the AME. I am dressed in civvy clothes and outwardly I look ridiculously healthy with a tan and legs that had chosen to work for the day. Having had my medical appointment I then visit George for a meeting that starts with a Command Interview. When you start working for an airline you sit in the right-hand seat as a First Officer and work your way up to Senior First Officer and then Captain which requires a number of interviews and tests and finally a command course. Becoming a captain is the pinnacle of a pilot's career and I am already part way through the process. That done, we finish with an exit interview whereby George explains how the company will look after me during my period of 'long term sick' and what they expect of me in return. It may be known as a low-cost airline but easyJet certainly isn't low cost when it comes to looking after its staff. I was to check in with George when something changed and other than that he would contact me occasionally to find out how I was doing. Simple. During the interview, George explains that the point of doing the command stuff as well is so that when I come back to work, I can go back into the command process where I have left off. I am starting to feel the enormity of what has just happened, and all the dots are starting to join up in my head all pointing towards a life in a wheelchair and I explain that there is a chance I may never walk again let alone fly. This is where George has a more profound influence over me than he will possibly ever know when he says again, "Emma, we are doing this so that WHEN you return to work you will be able to pick up where you left off." George had complete faith that everything would be ok, and I have always been grateful not only for that but for the many other times when I have turned to him for guidance and support and received exactly what I have needed at the time. I am fairly sure that George knows how grateful I am but just in case, George - thank you.

The next few weeks become a bit of a whirlwind and in some ways they seem endless as we cram so much into them. Now that my medical is suspended, I am free of work for probably the whole summer, and still mostly well enough to do all the things I would otherwise have been unable to because of work. We have tickets for Wimbledon for the third year in a row but this time on centre court and during that brilliant day we catch up with so many friends who are either there or live nearby. I spend time in Scotland at my home and with the children who are all at boarding school; I am never sure if they love being able to come home every night or find it to be a bit inconvenient that their school social lives have been interrupted by a parent who is desperate to see them. We attend the RAF Halton Summer Ball (the only time I have ever been to a ball with walking sticks which I needed to be sure I wouldn't fall over unexpectedly), we spend a day in London at Buckingham Palace with my best friend Bridget and our children who are by now home for the long summer, we visit my husband's family in Harrogate for the Tour de Yorkshire, we go to a Polo match, Royal Ascot, and then in the middle of it all, we move house.

One of the things about being a RAF wife is that you have to get used to the fact that you will move house several times in your life, possibly even overseas. All your garden plants will be in pots, and you basically have an opportunity every two or three years to chuck out a load of stuff you have accumulated and that turns out to be unnecessary and start again with a relatively tidy home. The downside of this is that you also have to say goodbye to people who have become good friends and your life support system in the knowledge that you now have to do the same thing all over again somewhere new.

On this occasion the move was not far, from Halton in Buckinghamshire to Bushey Heath just south of Watford, as my husband's job was moving from High Wycombe to Northwood. On the day of the move, I had been invited to the Farnborough Air Show by pilot friends at Stansted and the entire family decided that since I was next to useless anyway, I might as well go. I could drive and even walk most of the time but I couldn't do anything practical to help with the move so I drive away from the house at Halton for the last time knowing that I will be returning to a different house in Bushey that evening. I drive around to Farnborough taking my walking sticks with me but stubbornly choosing to wear chunky heels and leave the sticks in the car. I almost manage to pull this off - until I am walking towards the corporate tent we are being hosted in and my legs give way in front of the Boeing delegation. I find American men to be especially chivalrous and they rush over to help me to my feet when they see that I can't manage to pull myself up to standing. Conscious of the fact that it is only 11am and they may well think I am already drunk, I am quick to explain that I am in fact unwell and thank them profusely for their help. They respond by organising a Boeing golf cart which is put at my disposal for the rest of the day - I don't see them again but that small act of kindness meant so much when I was clearly struggling to accept that my fierce independence was being challenged to the extreme.

I return home after a really brilliant day when once again, I have bumped into people from across the industry and especially the

RAF who I haven't seen for a long time. I have even been able to return the favour of being invited to the air show in the first place by wangling a visit onto the American P-8 surveillance aircraft for me, Rich and Martin, my two friends, because the crew who are there to display it, happen to be pals of mine. We are not allowed into certain sections of the aircraft because of the nature of what it does but we are allowed into the flight deck, which is the bit, naturally, in which we are really interested.

Moving house complicates things slightly with all the investigations which are by now well underway. On being grounded I had asked the doctor to find the best neurologist in the country to see me no matter the cost on the basis that if I didn't get back to work in six months it was going to start costing me a lot of money in lost salary, and to cover ourselves, she put a referral request into the NHS as well. Within days she had come back to me telling me that she had found the best person for my situation and even better, there would be no charge for this. The medical practice I was registered with at Halton was military which was highly unusual as most military practices are for military personnel only. However, at Halton, they like to see 'dependents' as we were known then as it gives a broader mix of people for the medics who are undergoing their training there; we are not now allowed to be called 'dependents' because it is incorrect in the twenty first century to assume anyone is dependent on their partner; for the record I am mostly happy to depend on mine so I will stick with the phrase. The massive advantage of this from my point of view is that my wonderful doctor has been able to refer me through the military system to a Navy Commander named Matt Craner who was the chap all the RAF pilots were sent to with any neurological conditions. He is also an expert in his field - which is Multiple Sclerosis.

The first trip to see him is a bit surreal. He is based at Frimley Park Hospital in Surrey which is half NHS and half military, and my husband comes with me as in all honesty we are both a bit scared about what is happening and what it might mean. Things have been getting worse and our children are now home to witness it. On the plus side, they are all tall and strong and incredibly good natured about being asked to pick me up off the floor where I am now frequently finding myself with no ability to even pull myself up to standing. Once I'm down that's it, I have to stay there until I get picked up. It is so frustrating. Equally frustrating is the fact that I have no working shower in my house; something that may sound like a first world problem, but not something you expect in 2014, and I can only take a bath if someone is there to get me in and out of it.

We don't have to wait long, and he is brilliant. He carries out a few motor tests and asks a lot of questions and very quickly says the magic words, "It's not MS." I breathe a sigh of relief as I don't know if my mother will cope with having both children in wheelchairs (my brothers story appears at a different point in the book), but it does leave more questions. If not MS then what? Commander Craner thinks it may be Guillain-Barré syndrome and warns me not to google it as I won't like what I see. We have vaguely heard of GBS as it has been in the news but other than that we know nothing. What Commander Craner does say is that a google search will tell me that I should be admitted to hospital straight away, but he doesn't believe this to be necessary because he thinks it is quite mild. More tests are organised and over the course of the next few weeks of the summer, these lead to a changed diagnosis of Chronic Ideopathic Demyelenating Polyneuropathy otherwise known as CIDP - this is far too hard to say or explain so it becomes known as 'Jelly Legs' thanks to our good friend Charlie.

A good recovery from GBS is said to be that you will be able to walk unaided for ten metres. So, the fact that this has been ruled out is another relief, however CIDP falls into the relapsing/ remitting group of auto-immune triggered neurological diseases and is highly likely to render me unable to return to work. I feel completely disenfranchised and have lost my identity through this illness and also moving home. I have arrived at a new place where I know no-one, I am an airline pilot, but I can't work at the moment, I am a mother, but my children spend most of their time at boarding school 600 miles away, and until recently, I was a fit, strong, active person, who is no longer able to even walk out of the front door without falling down. This is not good, and I can't allow it to become the focus of my thoughts because I have to fight back and get better even if I can't make a full recovery; I have to get better than I am now.

I sincerely believe that people are sometimes placed in your life for a reason, and the people who came into my life next are some of the people without whom I wouldn't have known where to draw strength from in these seemingly dark days; people who are still some of my closest friends. When we moved into our house in Bushey Heath it was the first time we had ever lived somewhere that wasn't just RAF families. There were Army and Navy families as well, and there was also a strong Military Wives Choir. As luck would have it, there was a family living over the road from us who were RAF and were also extraordinarily warm, friendly and open people - we got on immediately, and within a couple of weeks, the houses either side of us had been filled by two army families (a lot of military moves happen in the summer - I think to accommodate schooling). Sara and Scotty on one side were expecting their first baby. Rebecca and Jamie on the other side had a little girl, and Rachel and Phil over the road had two children with another on the way. I was therefore a 'pro' with my three teenage children who provided an excellent source of babysitting when they were home for their long holidays - it is a fact of life that the more you pay for school, the less time your children will actually spend there. Sara was a trustee of the Military Wives Choirs organisation and Rachel was already a member of North London and so it was that I joined the choir when it regrouped in September and met an amazing bunch of ladies who I have laughed and cried harder with than most people I know and to whom I shall be forever grateful.

By the end of summer, Commander Craner had decided from all the tests I had that I needed a course of a blood by-product called Immunoglobulin to shut down my immune system and stop the madness that was going on in my body. This would mean spending a week on a drip as an outpatient at Frimley Park, and because the treatment was so expensive it would need the approval of the drugs board at the hospital, and this was likely to take a couple of months. However, time was not on my side, and one Friday towards the middle of August, I had a phone consultation during which I explained that whilst I had actually felt a lot better a week ago, I was now feeling weaker and had been falling over more frequently. This seemed to concern him, and by the end of that day he had called back to say, "I want you in on Monday, I have the approval I need to administer this treatment and I am concerned that things are progressing quickly."

There followed a round of questions to make sure we hadn't missed anything. He then said, "If you experience any further weakness or any shortness of breath over the weekend, you need to admit yourself to Watford General and tell them what you need." My reply must have seemed a bit half-hearted because he finished by saying, "Don't mess around with this Emma, I am concerned that this is progressing towards your heart and lungs and if that happens it could kill you." That was more sobering than the knowledge that on Monday morning I was going to have a lumbar puncture before the treatment began. I went to find my husband to tell him that my plans for the next week had just changed. Jim has often been described as being so laid back he might fall over, and his reaction to the news that I was about to spend a week going to and from Frimley was met with a classic Jim response, "Well I can take you on the first day and after that you can pretty much drive yourself can't you?" I must be clear here that this is not because he is an uncaring husband, but military men are used to having wives who are extremely independent, highly capable and don't need help with anything. As I write this I have so many stories in my head of the times when he wasn't there anyway, so I had to just get on with it. Like the time I was heavily pregnant with my first child, Jim was deployed somewhere, and I had a flat tyre. I knew how to change a wheel and the fact that the spare was mounted on the back door of our old Discovery didn't deter me. I was 'caught' by a friend's husband as he cycled back to work after lunch, trying to lift the massive wheel off the back of the car with my seven-month pregnant bump quite frankly getting in the way. Much to my inappropriate annoyance he stopped and insisted on changing the wheel for me while he gently told me off for being so stupid and not asking for help; clearly he was a legend, but it gives you an idea of why Jim was not used to having to change his plans. The hard stare I have come to perfect over twenty-six years of marriage must have been spot on as he very quickly started to work out the logistics of having three children at home, and how much of each day he would need to be at the hospital with me. We decided to call for back up and draft in my lovely Mum.

Monday morning was an early start, and the day began with a lumbar puncture. Having had three natural childbirths I can confirm that this is one of the most unpleasant things that any human can go through - add to that the fact that it was August (any doctor will tell you to NEVER have a procedure in August because it's when all the new medics are unleashed on real patients for the first time) and Commander Craner had not mentioned that he was on leave; he probably knew I would not have gone to the hospital if I had known. Now I'm no expert but I got the distinct impression that his replacement had possibly never done one of these before - or at least that it was her first solo attempt - as she explained to me what she was going to be doing, she had her eyes closed for most of the time, as if she was trying to remember what the text book said - although Jim was adamant that it was because she fancied him and was obviously distracted. It took three attempts to get the spinal fluid she needed to confirm that I was good to go and start the treatment. I did not enjoy this in any way whatsoever although I am obviously grateful to that doctor and hope she went on to achieve remarkable things.

What followed was a week of having what looked like mini aeroplanes sticking out of my arms as they tried to get immunoglobulin into my system, and two fantastic surprises. The first was that since I posted on Facebook that I was in Frimley and 'have aircraft stuck into my arm', I heard from two people who I hadn't seen for a long time. One of them was a lifelong friend, Kate, who was an Army officer and was moving house that week, she asked if she could borrow Jim as she was living close to Frimley, it was something of a relief for us both not to have to sit there making small talk all day as the magic liquid did its thing, and Kate got extra brute force to help move her furniture. The second was an old Uni friend called Olly who I hadn't seen for nineteen years since our wedding. He was in London visiting his dad and driving home past Frimley and would I like a coffee? It was so good to see him again and the years fell away as we sat talking and laughing our way through at least one bag of magic fluid if not two. It reignited a friendship and reminded me once again about what the important bits of life really are.

On Thursday, the penultimate day of treatment, Jim and I have been driving back and forth with him even admitting that he hadn't realised how hard it would be for me to drive with things sticking out of my arms as they were every night when I went home, not to mention how exhausting it was going through the treatment in the first place. For some reason I am in a private room on the ward and every twenty to thirty minutes one of the completely lovely nurses comes to check on me and my drip. I am not allowed to go to the loo or stand up and walk around on my own, so I ask Jim to help me, and as I get back into my wheelchair to be wheeled back to the bed I suddenly feel different. I feel as if a fog has lifted from my brain that I didn't know was there. And somehow, when it comes to the end of the day, I feel like walking is a bit easier and I can trust my legs a tiny bit more. I mention this to Jim, and it gives us a feeling of hope that things might just work out after all. Friday comes and the last day of treatment, and when I am checked over before being released, my blood pressure has dropped, the nurse suggests drinking lots of water, and so I do, it works, and I am free!

They say that timing is everything, and after this week of treatment, we decide to spend time at our home in Scotland while I gain strength and also, we need to prepare our children for the start of a new school year. Our son is about to start his

A Levels, and this is GCSE year for our oldest daughter, whilst our youngest has just turned thirteen and is making the move from prep school to the senior school. There is so much uniform to label before they go back, and I spend a lot of time on a sofa sewing in nametapes. This time at home is an essential part of my recovery. Our house is close to the sea and surrounded by farmland and forests and as I start to regain strength, I spend as much time on the beach as I can - I have always believed it is good for the soul and I need as much of that as I can get.

Eventually, school starts, and we have to pack up the house and go through the heart wrenching goodbyes that I hate so much and have never managed to get used to and make the long journey south to our other lives in Bushey Heath. Thanks, I suspect to the fact that I was fit and strong when I got sick, I make an astonishing recovery and sign up for a Princes Trust cycle ride from Buckingham Palace to Windsor Castle in September. Just before this, I have my first appointment with Commander Craner. I walk into his office, and he asks me how I am doing. I reply by doing a squat and saying, "Look what I can do!" He smiles, clearly delighted that he was right, and that he has managed to find a solution to something that was becoming a big problem. He is very happy with my progress but explains that my fitness level will have dwindled to almost nothing explaining that what has happened to my body in fitness terms is like being hit by a bus but without the injuries. He goes on to explain that my immune system had started to attack the myelin sheath around my spinal cord and that the resultant scarring had caused nerve damage which is why my big muscles had stopped working and I had lost all the sensation in my hands, feet and legs. He told me to take it slowly and be realistic about how long it would take to build up that kind of fitness again; so, I decided it probably wasn't a great time to mention the Princes Trust bike ride after all, I mean there was a sweeper bus, how hard could it be?!

I needn't have worried; I just pedalled at a speed I was comfortable with and cycled euphorically into Windsor in a respectable time having had a really nice outing on the bike with Jim alongside, but I was shocked when I first went back to the swimming pool. The 1000m I used to bang out with ease seemed far out of reach when I realised I couldn't even swim a length, and running was clearly going to take time to build up to. I did eventually get stronger through sheer stubbornness, and it has only really been in looking back on those months that I realise how bad things were, and especially at how close I came to not being here at all. I truly feel that I have been given a second chance at life and it completely changed the way I have approached everything that followed.

Chapter Four

Flightpath to Command

It is the 4th of July 2015; I wake up late having arrived home around 4am, to be greeted by my beloved daughters who are desperate to show me some unbelievably cute photos of a chocolate Labrador puppy wrapped in a fluffy white towel. Of course, they are showing me the photos because they want to see the puppies with the intention of bringing one home. I have made a big mistake. Having lost our black lab Monty at Easter, I have said to the children that we can't have another dog until after I have finished my command course, and the exact wording is important here, especially when negotiating with your children, because I didn't state that I had to pass the course, only that I had to come to the end of it. Children are gorgeous and adorable and make our lives complete, but they are also cunning and know where your weak points are. Mine are no exception and they are circling like sharks. I try to protest by appealing to their better natures feeling raw and battered about the events of the night before, but my children are ruthless, and they are not having any of it. "But Finckle (our eleven-year-old rescue mongrel) is lonely Mummy and anyway a puppy will cheer you up."

They know exactly how to manipulate both of us, and it doesn't take long for me to cave in and agree to go and look at the cute puppies. I am sure it is no surprise to hear that we come home with Poppy, who is gorgeous. In fact, we almost came home with one of her brothers too, but a line had to be drawn!

Poppy is indeed a brilliant distraction as I now have a 'management process' to go through at work. I also have to ask myself significant questions about my career and whether or not I am on the right path. In the run up to Jelly Legs I entered the Command Process. This is the path from sitting in the right-hand seat of an aircraft as a First Officer or Senior First Officer, to being on the left-hand side of the aircraft as the captain. Both pilots are equally capable of flying the aircraft and have been through the same exams, simulator checks, training course to fly a certain aircraft type (known as a Type Rating), but only one person can have overall responsibility for the aircraft and everyone on board, and that is the captain. When you learn to fly, you learn to fly in the left-hand seat of a training aircraft because you are the Pilot in Command, and consequently, when you learn to be a flying instructor as I had been, you have to learn to do everything from the right-hand seat so that you can teach people to fly in the left. The aircraft itself works in exactly the same way from either seat - but the buck stops with the captain and becoming one is what every pilot wants to be in the end.

By the time I lost my medical - almost a year ago to the day - I had completed most of the process that makes up the preliminary checking, and was at the point where I would be invited for an assessment in the simulator to see if I had the flying skills, the decision making ability, and the technical knowledge to proceed to the next stage which is the command course. It is a lengthy process for what I think are obvious reasons. Contrary to the hilarious comments from some of my RAF Navigator friends, they don't actually give out pilots licenses on the back of a cereal packet - it is hard work to get to the stage where you have completed the required training and reached the required standard to be in charge of a multi-million dollar aircraft, and the 200 plus passengers on board. It is often said that when you have completed a command course, you are the best you will ever be, not quite true but an idea of how high the standards are regardless of the airline you fly for.

After returning from being 'long term sick' I had to do a series of simulator checks and then spend a week flying around with a training captain to get me back to a point at which I could return into regular flying. During this time off I had also been granted a base transfer from Stansted to Luton. I started working at Stansted because it was near my parents, I was commuting from the Moray Firth in the North of Scotland, and the children sometimes had to come with me so that we could look after them in the holidays with both of us working. We partially solved this by sending them to Gordonstoun, chosen primarily because it was our local boarding school, but as life always has a funny way of changing any plans you have the audacity to make, they were there for six weeks before we were posted to High Wycombe and moved to RAF Halton just outside Wendover. It was the perfect location for me and an easy but long drive to work at Stansted. Luton made more sense on the basis that my husband's job was never going to move further east. I had made some brilliant friends at Stansted and have hilarious memories from being there, but it was time to move on.

Luton was friendly from the very beginning. I had already emailed the base captain to introduce myself and had become very used to working at different bases over the past five years, so it didn't take long to settle in and make new friends. I had been worried about landing at Luton and I didn't want my first experiences of what we called HMS Luton to be as the captain (Luton got that nickname due to it being on the top of a hill and more like an aircraft carrier than most airports we operated in to). Luton is just a runway like any other, but all airports have quirks and Luton has plenty of them. For a start, there is a steep bank with a road at one end of the runway which allows passengers to drive up to the car parks and the terminal, that's not unusual, many places are like that, Asturias in the north of Spain, and Jersey being two of my favourites. But Luton can also get foggy really quickly, in fact I have walked out to an aircraft on a crystal clear morning having seen the forecast of fog in the briefing pack and almost laughed it off, only to find that by the time we were ready to push back off our parking stand, it is so foggy, you can only just see far enough to taxi; you learn very quickly to take seriously what the "Met Man" says. (The Met Man is the weather forecaster and of course it can be a man or a woman!). Then there's the wind. Rumour has it that the anemometer (the instrument that measures the wind speed used by the Air Traffic Controller in the Airport Tower to tell you the wind speed and direction for landing and take-off) was put in place at the same time as a row of trees were planted. The trees subsequently, but not surprisingly, grew and provide a fair degree of shelter for the anemometer, so it was also the case that whatever the reported wind was on the day, you could expect to double it for your landing. There is also a hump part way down the runway, not to mention the fact that because Luton is on the edge of London airspace, it doesn't take much to have a challenging day. Luckily, pilots love a challenge and the way I dealt with landing at Luton in the early days was to simply pretend it was Stansted. After all, a runway is a runway and some of the perceived challenges are more psychological than physical.

So here I was at Luton, having just returned from six months off with an illness that tried and failed to kill me, ready to throw myself at everything my job had to offer. I had been told that I could pick up the command process where I had left off and that once I was ready all I needed to do was hit GO. I gave myself time to settle back into the day-to-day routine of flying, and after a couple of months I felt that I was good to go again, so I spoke with my base captain, who agreed to put the wheels in motion. Everything was going well. I had a slight niggle in my back, but most days I could stretch it out. I figured that this was largely because I wasn't doing anything like the activity I had been before I got sick, and it was normal to have some aches and pains when you return to exercise after a period of inactivity.

The next stage of the process is known as the Command Assessment sim, for this I was sent to Gatwick where I was rostered to be tested along with a lovely chap but who my heart went out to when he failed his part of the sim. I tried to help him out as much as I could, but you are not supposed to help too much and eventually the instructor, who is able to speak to each pilot individually through their headset system, asked me to stop. I was gutted as I had a feeling then that he would fail but I still had my own assessment to get through. A high number of people fail their first attempt at this simulator session, it is a tough knock but better to find out earlier rather than later if you are not ready. Thankfully I was ready, I passed the sim check and the next stage was to wait to be rostered on to a command course which was expected in the next couple of months. In the meantime, I could sit back, relax and enjoy the journey.

As I had been working hard to return to fitness, as well as to the flight deck, I had committed to taking part in a couple of sporting events. The first was the Princes Trust Palace to Palace cycle ride from Buckingham Palace to Windsor Castle which took place two days after my first check up with my neurologist who confirmed I was well on the way to recovery, but also warned me that my fitness levels could be expected to be on the floor. I completed this in a time I was happy with; I was simply happy to complete it given what I had been through in the previous six months.

The second event was rather more ambitious. Each of our children spent time on a service project for which they needed to raise money, around £3,000, and my son had come up with a plan to do a sponsored bike ride from Waterloo Station in London to Waterloo in Belgium; he and my husband both have a great interest in military history and only my husband had been to Waterloo before, so the decision was made. Honestly, my main motivation was to be able to cycle up to that historic mound singing at the top of my voice that I was 'finally facing my Waterloo' but I pretended it was all about the journey. Our friend Charlie decided he would join the party and so the four of us set off with one of us driving our car as a support vehicle and the others cycling. It was a fantastic and epic journey that warrants a book all by itself. When I did finally cycle down the approach road, I was too knackered to speak let alone sing, but we had done it, and it was brilliant. We had lunch, got in the car, and drove home with a squeaky moment at Calais when my husband realised that his passport had expired. None of our passports had been checked on the way over, thankfully avoiding what would have been a bit of an exchange of opinions, or more exactly quite a lot of micky taking that we had all checked ours. Now we, or more precisely he, was stuck in France! On this occasion it was Jim's lucky day because when he was asked to show identification and was able to produce his military ID card, a couple of phone calls were made, and we were on our way.

This bike ride was amazing but over the next few weeks I found out why it is never a good idea to undertake a 300-mile bike ride after a serious illness, and with no training! My back was starting to cause me more problems and some days it was painful to walk. By now I was on leave and waiting for my command course to begin so I figured I would get the course out of the way and then get my back sorted. When you have your eyes on a prize for long enough, you don't always make the same decisions you would with the benefit of hindsight, and so I carried on.

There were three days of ground school at the start of the course, and it was a real delight to find that one of my course mates from my type rating was on the course with me. Joe is a lovely man, and it was good to see his face again as it had been six years since we all arrived at a hotel in the New Forest to start our airline training. It was going to be an enjoyable time. We were all booked in to the crew hotel in Crawley but for those of us who were based at one of the London bases this was only for the days we were actually rostered to work and I found it disruptive to have to pack up and go home in the middle of the course while the rest of them stayed on in the hotel - this has since changed but it is strange to be in the middle of a really intense course and then go back to being mummy for a few days.

The simulator part of the command course is made up of six sim sessions - three training sessions and three checking sessions. The first two sims went well. My sim partner and I were comfortable working together, but my back was getting worse. In fact, on the third day, it was so distracting that I considered leaving the course, but once again I thought that if I could just get through the next session I would then have a few days off during which time I could sort out my back for the final push to the end. Actually, the decision ended up being made for me because I failed the sim, passed the resit the next day but only just, and my instructor commented on me limping when we got back to the hotel. The next morning, I woke from a pain filled sleep and was terrified to find that I couldn't move. I somehow managed to get dressed but it took me an hour to get downstairs for breakfast where I met my instructor and told him I couldn't continue. He agreed wholeheartedly, and pretty heroically, he organised painkillers from the hotel, spoke to the airline on my behalf to explain what had happened and having spoken to 111 and been told to go to A&E because of the pain, he arranged a lift as well.

I was off the course and had to go home, but I couldn't drive so I called my husband and asked him to come to the rescue. He was at Lords watching cricket, and it was going to take him a while to work out how to get to Crawley and come to my rescue, so I had plenty of time to pack.

I had been prescribed some super strong drugs and was quite happy to chill out in the hotel for the day. My training captain, Carl, phoned me in the afternoon to ask if I wanted a trip out for a cup of tea, he was going anyway and thought I might enjoy the distraction. We talked about everything but work and it was one of the many occasions throughout this process when I was shown great kindness by people who didn't need to go out of their way, and to whom I remain immensely grateful.

With anything to do with health, there is a process to go through. Firstly, I had to sort out my back. I saw my GP and a physio and was put on a waiting list for an MRI scan for a suspected prolapsed disc. Ten days later I was given the all clear to go back to work and I was then re-scheduled for the rest of the simulator sessions with a refresher sim to start with. By now the rest of my course had moved on and they were in the flying stage of their training. One by one they sent messages to our WhatsApp group to say that they had successfully passed and were now captains - I was proud of all of them but especially Joe because we had started out type ratings together and had that 'Command Course Connection' that any captain will tell you is a really strong bond.

I still had the rest of the simulator training to go though and now I had to do this with a real First Officer sitting in the right-hand seat. It went well and I was actually starting to enjoy it and feel more like a captain.

My final simulator session was rostered to be what is known as an E slot on 3rd July - the E slot is hated by most pilots whether they are trainers or not because it runs from 2200 to 0200, which means you start work at 2030 and finish anywhere between 0230 and 0300 depending on how long your debrief is. The failure I was given is one of the most complex failures there is, but nevertheless one that I should have been able to manage, and although I made some sound decisions, it was clear to the examiner that I was out of my depth. The First Officer was sent home after a very quick debrief and it was just me and the examiner, a lovely man who I knew from Luton and who I am still friends with. We went through the motions of debriefing what had just happened. I was still hopeful that there was a chance I might have scraped through but eventually he said the words no one ever wants to hear, "I'm really sorry Emma, I can't pass you, I have to put it down as a fail." I don't know what he said next, all I could hear was the word FAIL, after forty-two years of never failing at anything I had turned my hand to, I had failed the course that I had been working towards for the last six years. It was crushing and I know now that the examiner was just as gutted to have to give me that news because he knew how hard I had fought to get here.

Having discussed the possible options, it was time to drive home, utterly defeated and crying for most of the way, wondering how I was going to tell my friends and family that I had completely let them all down. I got home and tried to creep into bed quietly but my husband, who has always had complete faith in me, was so excited that I was home after what he thought would have been a pass was already awake, and when he hugged me and told me it would all be OK I cried myself to sleep in his arms, and woke up much later in the morning to my children, showing me photos of a cute puppy wrapped in a towel. There is nothing better than slightly evil children to remind you that self-pity is pointless!

There was a fall out from all of this because whilst I had not passed the command course, I was also no longer qualified to operate as a first officer. Before I could go back to work, I would have to spend more time in the simulator to either have another go at repeating that final check, or to re-train back into the right-hand seat. Prior to any of that being decided I had to have a meeting with the Head of Training at easyJet HQ. My base captain advised me to go in uniform and the meeting was friendly and relaxed and more about me being given the opportunity to talk about what had gone wrong than the sort of rollocking I was expecting. The Head of Training, Dave, rounded up the meeting by saying, "It's clear you can pole it around the sky, but I need to

GROUNDED

satisfy myself that you are going to be safe out on the line with hundreds of passengers on board."

I got it. No airline can afford for there to be any doubt about the people they put in the flight deck, and I completely understood that they had to consider what to do with me now. It didn't take too long for the answer to come, Dave phoned me a few days later and said, "What I'm about to say to you means that you won't listen to anything else that follows so write down my phone number and call me back tomorrow when you have processed everything." I knew then that I was to return to the right-hand seat, I had failed, and it was over. Dave had tried to think of so many different ways that they could make it happen, I believe because I was well known as being a hard worker, a good egg, and the circumstances that surrounded and contributed to my failure, but it was finished.

It took several weeks to find space in the simulator for me to go back to work and I felt battered and broken by what had happened, so much so that I questioned whether or not I should ever fly again. We took advantage of me being off work during the summer and booked a holiday to Malta.

In the days running up to this escape to our own personal paradise, I go through all the emotions of what I suppose is a kind of grief. I have lost something I held dear, not a loved one but something that had been taking up a large part of my life - and I need to allow myself time to work through the emotions that this has brought out. The feeling of humiliation is overwhelming although, it appears, no one other than me believes that at all. I decide I need to think about whether or not I am going to return to work; is this actually what I am supposed to be doing, all those missed birthdays, weddings, the weekends the children get off from school when I don't get to spend the time with them... what's it all for now? After a few days of mulling this over I decide that I have worked too hard and more importantly my family have made too many sacrifices for me to just give up and walk away, it's only a failed course for goodness sake, I know I can fly, I am just not ready for the enormous responsibility of command. Maybe it is time for me to move on from easyJet. Maybe this lifestyle is not the one I should be pursuing. I make calls to friends I have in the corporate aviation world, as well as a friend at Air Tanker, the civilian arm of the RAF based at Brize Norton. Maybe there are openings there. Everyone sympathises greatly with my soul searching but there just aren't any opportunities and it occurs to me that no one is going to want to employ someone with a failed command course under their belt - it doesn't exactly scream 'hire me'.

We have never been to Malta before, and we spend twelve glorious days completely isolated from everyone and everything in a fortified farmhouse on the northern Island of Gozo followed by a few days in the capital Valletta. It is always hot there, but we find ourselves there in a heatwave which means that all we can do is lie in the sun and occasionally flop into the pool. It is good for the soul, time to heal, and precious time with our growing children.

I instantly fall in love with Malta. Apart from the heat and sunshine which I am well known for craving (my friends know that if it's a sunny day they won't find me inside because I have a hammock and why would I be inside when I can be outside in that!), the farmhouse we are staying in is completely enchanting. A mile or so outside the village of Gharb, it is up a small hill, and the grounds are completely enclosed by thick walls. The hill might be small, but it is steep enough to challenge the minuscule car that we have hired. Somehow, I am married to a man who genuinely believes that when on holiday, we should hire the smallest car available that will take five people, even though the next size up is only an extra tenner - this happens every single year on holiday, and every single year, we squeeze ourselves into the equivalent of a Nissan Micra along with all our luggage and drive, to wherever we are staying. This was slightly easier when the children were small, but they are teenagers the size of fully grown adults. All three of them tower over me to the point where I have to stand on the stairs if I ever want to try, and fail every time, to exert any sort of authority whatsoever. So, when we arrive for the first time at the farmhouse, the tiniest car in Malta will not only refuse to go up the hill with us in it, but it also can't manage with just our bags on board! We unload the car laughing at poor Jim for being so tight and carry our bags up the small hill and through the front door. It is an oasis of calm, with a beautiful pool, bougainvillea and devils' ivy growing up the walls and as we later find out, a resident chameleon. We have never seen one before and this one casually lounges around in the bushes at the edge of the pool providing us with as much entertainment as we can cope with in the forty-degree heat - even watching him sitting still, although fascinating, is exhausting.

Malta is lovely and I also fall for Gozo and its clear blue water, ancient catacombs, and amazing history, so much so that I suggest to Jim that there might be a job at Air Malta, and I could look into transferring. Jim is a kind and patient man so even though he knows there isn't really an ice lolly hope in hell of this ever actually happening, he humours me. "Why not, you could look into it at least," he says. I don't even think about what he would do with his career or how we would keep the children in school but my answer to my wondering comes a few days later when the headline in the Maltese newspaper that is delivered to the apartment we have rented in Valletta reads, 'AIR MALTA ANNOUNCES REDUNDANCIES' - apparently the airline has been heavily overcrowded with staff for years and is now in trouble. My question is answered, and Malta returns to its rightful place in our lives of 'amazing holiday destination' rather than 'potential new home'.

Eventually we have to return home to face the music and one Sunday while I am waiting for my return-to-work simulator sessions, I tell my friend and pastor Helen about what's happened and how rubbish I feel because of it. She listens to everything I have to say and puts her arm around me and says, "Emma this won't define you, but rather it will REFINE you and when the time is right, and you get your command, you will be a much better captain for it." Helen was right, and I have since told her how important her words were and how much I needed to hear them.

In the end, the return-to-work training is a breeze - there is no pressure anymore, I am just returning to a job I have been doing for five years - I know what I am doing and the expectation of every single one of the training captains I meet is that I will get another go in six months. They have all looked at my training record and all the notes that have been made and this is what they have concluded.

Returning to the flying side of my job is good fun but has its sticky moments. The most potentially awkward is one morning in the crew room at Luton. I am standing at the briefing table with my training captain talking through the day before the rest of the crew arrive. Several people congratulate me on what they assume must be the flying part of my command training. I put a brave face on it, smile and say I didn't quite make it, which eventually morphs into, 'they realised they couldn't actually afford me in the end' - always looking to find something funny to say to alleviate my colleague's discomfort and my own. Their words of sympathy are met with the reaction I have decided to show the world, it doesn't matter, and I will just do it next time instead. The fact that I don't whinge, moan or try to blame anyone else is not only the honest approach, but also one that wins me the respect of my colleagues, and one that I have come to terms with over the last few weeks. Thanks to Jelly Legs, I realise there are more important things in life than work and the status and income that may bring, and I am still healthy, still have a family that loves me and still have a job that I love even if I am in a different seat than I had hoped.

I still haven't been told by the company how long I will have to wait for another go at command and I am flying with a training captain called Rod who I get on well with; he is ex-RAF and his family originally comes from a place called Pluscarden which is not far from where I live in Scotland so we always have things to talk about, and have flown together before. He is kind and gentle with me about what has happened, and we have a good day out. The final two flights of the day are to Belfast and back and I am the pilot flying on the way there. While we are on the ground at Luton, an email arrives from the company telling me that the decision is that I must wait a year before I can try again, and I am so upset I can't tell Rod what the email says but ask him instead to read it. I am fighting back tears but determined I am not going to cry in front of such a lovely and extremely professional man. He asks me if I want to offload myself and feels really sorry for me over what he considers to be a relatively harsh decision but all that will mean is that I have to walk through a crowded terminal building and drive home feeling miserable while ruining someone else's evening when they are called to replace me. I choose to stay, and Rod supports this understanding as I do that the best thing here is to get back on the horse and ride it.

As we roll down runway 08 at Luton to take off towards Belfast, a small trickle of tears escapes, but I am not going to be defeated by this, I have regained my mojo, and I will do what it takes to succeed.

On hearing the news of how long I must wait, there are some who suggest I should appeal the decision, and I do consider it, but after a very honest conversation with George, who so confidently told me I would be back after my illness, I decide to let it go, accept the decision, and get on with my life. I choose to enjoy the job I know and love, sitting more or less fat, dumb and happy in the right-hand seat with minimal responsibility, watching, learning, and making sure that when the chance comes around again, I am truly ready.

As I meander through the next few months, and with the benefit of hindsight I can see that the biggest mistake I made was thinking I was ready to go for command before I really was; I was so focussed on the final goal that I couldn't see what was happening all around me and in the end, although it was a really tough knock, I still believe the correct decision was made and I became a better captain for it.

When the opportunity comes around again it is almost like Groundhog Day as I have to repeat the command assessment simulator check, which I sit with my sim partner Matt who is one of the merry band of brothers on my new command course.

By now we have moved from Bushey Heath just south of Watford, to North Hykeham on the outskirts of Lincoln, and my commute to Luton is now a much longer one. When we got married I always said to Jim that I never wanted to live in Lincolnshire and if he ever moved there I wouldn't go with him. I was so adamant about this that when he was offered promotion from Squadron Leader to Wing Commander with a posting to RAF Waddington, he seriously considered turning it down; in fact, he was fairly adamant that he wasn't going to accept it because he knew I wouldn't move there. I am not excited in any way about moving to a place that I knew as being always wet, miles from anywhere we needed to be (Luton or our children in Scotland or any of our parents) and also miles from the sea. I am starting to get tired of moving around as well - this will be our ninth move in twenty years of being married which is actually a really small number for a military family. Most people only stay in one place for two years and we have been lucky with some long postings, but bouncing from Scotland to New Zealand, to England, back to Scotland and then back to England without the children, whilst it has its fun moments, is starting to wear us down. I miss home and the house we built, and I want to go back there. For now, it is not an option, so I convince Jim that he has to accept the promotion and we will make it work. A few weeks later we find ourselves moving into what is admittedly a very lovely new house six miles away from my best friend Bridget. Like most military wives I have got used to making the best of every new posting and as always when I declare that I don't want to go somewhere, I find lots to be thankful for.

The course content hasn't changed since the last time. I feel so much more relaxed going into it. Once again, my course mates are an excellent group of people and we quickly settle into a routine of meeting up for dinner each night, working together through the things we need to get our heads around and actually start to really enjoy it. My sim partner is Toby, who is only a few years older than my son; he is really sharp and also brilliant fun. Fun is not something you would normally associate with a command course, but we have it in bucketloads. Every night it seems to be someone's birthday when we go out for dinner so that we get ice cream puddings with sparklers and the whole restaurant sings happy birthday. I still have my Mexican hat from Chiquitos although I'm not completely convinced I can remember how many Tequilas were consumed. The highlight of the social side of the course is the day we spend Go-Karting. Despite having been born and brought up in Essex and driving my little Ford Fiesta way too fast around country roads late at night, I am not a brave go-kart driver, and my course mates don't just laugh when they race off ahead of me, they then lap me, one of them twice! I am pathetic, but by the time we finish my face hurts from laughing so much and I am convinced that this group bonding session is instrumental in our success as all but one of us sails through the rest of the course. When one struggles I spend time talking to them, and the whole course pulls together to try and support him, all feeling gutted when he has to leave. I know only too well what that feels like and remind myself that although it is hard to lose one of our number, we all have to move on.

Passing the final simulator check feels even better for being the second time around, and now it is time to go home and celebrate, there is still the flying phase of the training to come but I am looking forward to it. I am ready.

Returning to Luton with a successful course under my belt is a great feeling and my training captains (who now sit in the right-hand seat as I am now in the left) are almost as pleased as I am because they know how hard I worked to be there and many of them praise the dignity with which I handled it. At last, it is time for my final check ride and training captain Mark is my man for the day. I have a real First Officer in the right-hand seat and Mark sits in the jump seat behind us. We have a good day out and by complete chance we are flying in A319 G-EZEH, which I consider to be my own personal aircraft because it has my initials at the end. When we land at Luton for the final time, it is dark, and Mark says nothing until we have shut the engines down on stand. I fill in the aircraft's logbook, sign it, say goodbye to the passengers and when I return to the flight deck Mark shakes my hand and gives me a hug as he says, "Congratulations Emma, you have passed. You are a captain, and I couldn't be prouder."

I can't keep the smile off my face and the whole crew are excited as they have known all day that it is my check ride. There is a lot of paperwork to fill in before I can go home, and I now have some days off to let it all sink in. There is a large glass of wine waiting for me when I get there and Jim and I celebrate the fact that after all we have been through starting with the command process being interrupted almost three years before, I am now Captain Emma Henderson, and nothing can take that away from me.

Hindsight is a wonderful thing and although this journey was tough, it was one that taught me a considerable amount about myself and about the spirit of my colleagues. From line captains I flew with, to my friends I had trained with, right up through the training department to the Head of Command training, there wasn't a single person who was anything other than kind, supportive and encouraging. I am convinced that this had a lot to do with the way in which I chose to handle defeat with grace, learn the lessons that were there to be understood, and allow myself to be on the receiving end of the help that was offered from these colleagues and wingmen of mine. All too often we may think we can struggle on and manage, or we may think there is no one to turn to, but we seldom need to navigate alone through difficulty, and the aircrew spirit that enveloped me was going to show itself again, in so many amazing ways and on a much greater scale, just a few years later.

Chapter Five

Oh, the Glamour

Pilot life might seem glamorous to some people, but I am sure it is no surprise to learn that the reality is often very different. For the average traveller, waking up in the middle of the night to arrive at an airport on time for the annual holiday is a mild inconvenience and very much a means to a delicious end involving a beach or a ski resort, lakes, mountains and hopefully a cold G&T. For more frequent travellers it might be a lucrative business deal awaiting them at the other end. For pilots, this is our bread and butter. A 0600 departure to Ibiza means arriving at the airport in time to check in at 0500 - one hour before departure and like a lot of our passengers, we drive to the airport. Public Transport links are good in places, but you are more likely to be crowned King or Queen than to find any sort of regular and reliable service between the towns and villages we live in, and an airport, at the times of day we need to travel.

Unlike passengers, pilots, cabin crew, and all other airport workers, don't have the option of deciding to go for Valet Parking, 'because it will be a nice treat when we get home, and we get a free shuttle.' Airlines are customers of airport owners and as such must pay for luxuries such as car parking and for this reason, the staff car park will be located somewhere in the next county, as far away from the terminal as possible to still just about define it as airport parking. This means either taking a crew bus or a walk that can be as much as twenty or thirty minutes. By the way, the timetable for a crew bus seems to operate on the basis that it always pulls out of the car park just as you are parking your car and the next one will be here after you are supposed to have checked in. Being a predominantly health-conscious bunch, and ever mindful of the permanent damage sitting down all day does to our bodies, many of us will walk and enjoy a few moments of air and peace before the working day begins, arriving at our terminal buildings either completely drenched or completely overheating because we always forget how far it is and how heavy our bags can become even over a shortish distance!

In most airports, the crew must clear security before reaching 'the office', and in many places, there is no longer even an office; the arrival of the much longed-for company iPad (other tablets are available) has brought with it the demise of the bustle of the crew room, and therefore any chance of ever seeing someone you might know to say hello to. As crew, we go through the same security procedures as anyone else who needs to be airside at an airport, but in the UK this is usually in a different location from the actual terminal building. In reality, this means removing your coat, uniform jacket, watch, belt and boots, as well as your company and personal iPad, your company and personal phones, anything electrical like a phone charger, as well as liquids.

Most pilots will carry a 'night stop kit' comprising of tiny bottles of shampoo, shower gel, deodorant and toothpaste as well as emergency pants and socks for that unscheduled stop down route; in fairness, in twelve years, I only ever had three or four of these occasions, and of course, they were on days when I had thrown caution to the wind and not packed my night stop kit. Assuming you don't set the alarm off on the way through the arch or are selected for a random test, you are free to go and pack all this stuff back into your bag, which as most passengers know, is always harder to fit everything in compared to when you packed before leaving for the airport. You get dressed for the second time that day and make your way to the crew room or increasingly, direct to the aircraft. It is the same procedure that passengers go through and quite right too - the only difference is that we do this EVERY SINGLE DAY of our working lives. Glamorous thus far it isn't.

I always felt that getting through security was a bit like a sausage factory and sometimes, even getting through to the other side was a bit exhausting, and that is only the start of the day, whether it is 4 am, or 8 pm ready for a night flight. When I started working for an airline, the next part of the day was the civilised and sociable bit - head to the crew room, check-in for the flights, print the flight plans off, check the weather, meet the crew, talk about the day, ask how everyone is feeling which is important regardless of the time of day, make a fuel decision, phone it through to the fueller, find out where the aircraft is and then walk out to it using the underground warren of corridors where only airport workers are allowed. By the time I stopped working as a captain, some fundamental things had changed - the main one being that having cleared security, we would more often than not head straight to the aircraft and the first one there would open up and wait for everyone else - briefing on board as it is known is the future - think of the money that saves in valuable terminal space instead of having a crew room, however, it removes the ability to get to know your crew for the day which is so much more vital than some people think but should be obvious to all concerned.

On days when we are not rostered for flying duty, we are on standby, either at home when we must be able to be at work within ninety minutes, or at the airport so that we are ready to go immediately, and sometimes the standby callouts involve moving around the network as a passenger to carry out 'rescue' flights.

Twice when I was at Stansted I was called out to be flown in a private jet to bring an aircraft back to the UK - this was quite glamorous - it is the only time I have ever flown like that and even though we were in uniform and at work, it was fun. On one occasion, the pilot was also a friend, and we were being flown to Ajaccio as a whole crew to fly an aircraft to Lyons and then be flown back to the UK again. The Citation C12 we were travelling in, had six seats - exactly the right number for our crew, and came fully stocked with food and drink and we could have anything we wanted. Because we were on duty the champagne was rightly, but sadly, off-limits; everything else was fair game and we had a lot of fun pretending that we were living the high life rather than being ferried to work in what was essentially an expensive taxi. Our aircraft are limited to 39,000 feet, so when the Citation captain asked if we had any preferred cruising altitude, I was excited to find out that we could go up to 45,000 feet, "Let's go all the way up then," I said, and was like a kid in a sweet shop when the onboard display showed we had reached that cruise level – 6,000 feet higher than I had been before, almost a mile higher at 8.5 miles up and the difference is astonishing. At 39,000 feet (or Flight Level 390 as it is called) you can see the curvature of the earth but at FL450 it is much more pronounced and the sky above it is so much darker. It was an experience I will never forget and enjoyed, even with all the messing around at the other end to take over from the French crew who had picked up a delay and gone out of hours. We flew their aircraft, and passengers back to Lyon, hopped back onto our private jet which had shadowed us from Ajaccio and were flown back to Stansted again. This time, as we were going off duty we were allowed to take the champagne, but not drink it until we were home. By the time I did arrive home, at 4 am, it was a bit late so that was saved for another day.

These trips were so few and far between that I only had one other, also at Stansted, and this time it was just me and Captain Jeremy who were flown to Lyons to wait for an aircraft that was on its way back to Luton, but again, so delayed that the flight deck needed to be replaced. I had flown with Jeremy before but that trip was when we became friends because we had so much time to talk to each other - a friendship that meant that we were invited to his wedding a few years later, one of the coolest I have ever been to - I have never before or since been to a wedding where the groom flies his bride from the church to the reception escorted by a Harvard, a beautiful plane that we all got to pose alongside; pilots love to pose more than anything and I'm happy to take that hit!.

On the flip side of the coin are all the trips I was called out for to either spend a few days down route in Lisbon, Lyon or Madrid, and it was one of these callouts that found me checking in at Luton as a passenger on a flight to Lisbon where I was to be working for a couple of days. I enjoyed these trips because the crew hotel was in the city which made it easy to explore before or after work. I always travelled in civvy clothes because there is nothing worse than being in uniform and someone deciding that you are the person who can answer all their questions, and their gripes, about the airline - don't get me wrong, I love talking about my job but not necessarily for three hours on the way to work. Because I travel a lot up and down the country, I have lounge access, it just makes life easier for me as a commuter. When you spend more than half your life in an airport or on a plane, small things like that matter, so I was quite chilled out having had my 'free' food and drink in the Priority Lounge in the terminal and I was happily minding my own business in the speedy boarding crew, having checked a bag with all my uniform into the hold, when my work phone rang. One of the 'perks' of being a captain is a mobile phone - in this case, a purely functional Nokia - it is the opposite of a smartphone and despite being able to fly a $150 million passenger jet, I don't know any captain who can work out how to use it for anything much more than a basic phone call - which is, I suspect, the whole point. It is Crewing calling. In fact, it is 'Grumpy Stuart', a gruff Yorkshireman who takes no prisoners, a good thing as his job is mostly phoning people in the middle of the night and asking them to get up and go to work because they are needed from their standby. Not everyone is nice about this way of being woken up and although Stuart and I have disagreed in the past, I am always polite and friendly on the phone because all those in a similar role are only doing their jobs, and you never know when you are going to need them to remember you as being someone they might want to help.

Today, Stuart is not grumpy, he is positively cheerful, which can only mean he wants me to do something; I later learned that he was a complete teddy bear most of the time! "So, Emma, when you get to Lisbon, I have a delayed Geneva I need you to operate, please". OK, no problem, I was only going to the hotel anyway so I might as well go to Geneva on the way. "There's just one thing," Stuart continues, I need you to jump straight off your flight and straight onto the Geneva flight. We will arrange for someone to collect your baggage and you can collect it from the crew room later on." Although I have checked a bag into the hold, pilots NEVER travel for work without their flight bag - it's just too difficult to replace everything it contains if it should go missing - so in theory I have everything I need to carry out the flight. I have my passport (obviously), my licence, my headset, and a pen; I don't need more than that. There is one tiny obstacle though and that is I am not in uniform. It is not unusual for the flight crew to operate out of uniform, and I have heard of people doing it before, but I am wearing a strappy top, a skirt and sandals which isn't ideal flight deck clothing. I explain to Stuart that I am in civvies and as expected, he says cheerfully, "That's ok, you can fly in those." They must really need this flight to go. "What's the delay to the flight at the moment," I ask innocently, there is a pause before Stuart confesses that it will be a five-hour delay by the time I arrive. I laugh, there is NO WAY I am operating a five-hour delayed flight in a skirt and t-shirt, I need my uniform. I say, "No problem, leave it with me and I will phone you as soon as we land in Lisbon." Damn it, how am I going to get my bag out of the hold. Luckily, I have only got tiny toiletries packed in it and it's quite a small bag so there is no reason why it couldn't go in the cabin, I just need to get it. I have a secret and very valuable weapon; the other thing we never travel without is our ID cards, worn on a lanyard around our necks, they open doors all over Europe, figuratively and literally. Being based at Luton, I know the ground crew not just from working but also from all the flights I take up and down the country, I explain to them that I need my bag from the hold and why, and they let me through to speak to the captain (it's his aircraft, it's his call) and after a quick search (helped by the fact that my luggage is bright red with flowers on it) I have my bag containing my uniform in the cabin and there will be no unnecessary delay.

I phone Stuart once we land and tell him I have a plan and will be in uniform and on the next aircraft within half an hour so he can get the wheels in motion to get the passengers on board and I will join them as soon as I can. Once all of my travelling companions have left the aircraft I lock myself into the forward loo and change from summer traveller to working captain. Anyone who knows how tiny those loos are can appreciate that this is not that straightforward, it's a tight space and easy to keep knocking the flush button; a shock the first time it happens to say the least.

Finally, I am changed and ready to take the delayed passengers to Geneva. I don't speak much Portuguese, but my First Officer is local and does a brilliant job of advising them that we will get there as fast as we can and telling them all they can have a free drink once we are airborne. It helps a little and we manage to make up some time on the way; it is still a big delay but not as big as it could have been. Stuart sends me a message to say thank you and the next day he is on duty again when my taxi doesn't arrive at the hotel to take me to work, he couldn't have been nicer, sorted out the taxi for me and was so charming I instantly forgave him for the time he had been very grumpy to me years before. That aircraft toilet is one of the least glamorous places in which I have changed for work, but I am glad that the last time I spoke to Stuart, we laughed and were kind. I am glad because Stuart passed away at the end of 2020. I had left the airline by then, but I know he will be missed, and I have no doubt at all that he was one of the best on the crewing team.

These occasions were few and far between, but always memorable, and sometimes it was the other way around where we would operate a jet to an airport and spend the rest of the day coming home or have an overnight stay and then a flight home the next day.

It was on one of these protracted journeys home that I first learned about putting pepper on strawberries; if you haven't tried it, do give it a go, it makes them even more delicious. Along with Captain Kev, who calls me Relish after the Henderson's Relish made in Sheffield where he is from, I was sent to take an empty aircraft to Milans Linate airport. I have been there many times since, but this was the first occasion I had ever been and Kev, being the lovely chap that he is, let me fly us there. There is no direct link between Linate and Stansted so the way we were to travel home was to take a flight from Linate to Copenhagen, and then from Copenhagen to Stansted. It sounded exciting at first, but it was a 6 am start and a very long day. By the time we were finally on the flight back to Stansted, we were still laughing but starting to flag a little. I always packed far too much food for airport standbys which was a good thing on this occasion; I had a whole punnet of strawberries which I shared with Kev. "Try them with pepper," he said. I laughed and said, "Yeah right - like I would fall for something like that," assuming he was trying to trick me, but no, he was serious, I tried it, and they were amazing!

I was flying with Kev again later that year to Tallinn. It was winter and one of the very few times I have landed on a runway made of snow. Since it was my flight back to Stansted, it was my walk around and the apron was covered with de-icing fluid making it treacherous. I managed to get all the way around the aircraft before I slipped on the sticky yellow gloop covering myself in a mixture of that and slush - I was completely soaked. Once Kev had established that I was OK - we both laughed that only I could do something so completely stupid - you can imagine the look on Kev's face when I told him that I was sorry but I was going to have to take my trousers off to try and dry them out a bit - I couldn't sit in a sticky puddle all the way back to Stansted - a three-hour flight - Kev was a good sport and took it in his stride - even more so when I pointed out that I was also wearing thick black tights as it was so cold - so really it would be like wearing leggings. It was admittedly strange flying with my trousers hanging over the back of my chair drying but needs must! To add to the ridiculousness of this day, as we got back into Stansted, we got a message from Ops to ask us to take the aircraft to Gatwick. There had been a lot of heavy snow in the UK and so many aircraft were out of position they needed as many as possible at Gatwick to protect the first wave in the morning. Sticky trousers aside we were both feeling fit, so we agreed and had a fun 15-minute flight over a snowy nighttime London typically arriving at a Gatwick that was a ghost town. There was no one around and we waited for almost an hour to park up and leave the aircraft. At this point we didn't know how we were getting home and with my trousers by now dry and back on me, we left the aircraft and headed for the crew room to find out. Kev had a taxi booked back to Stansted while I was in a crew hotel for the night - there was no way I was going to stay in Gatwick overnight with only a filthy set of clothes to my name - and Kev called crewing to find out why. It was something to do with crew hours but he fought my corner and told them they had to allow me to travel back to Stansted with him - they agreed thankfully and we ended up in a minicab on the snowiest M25 I have ever witnessed with only one barely open lane - the cab driver drove like a bat out of hell and it was scary - and Kev (my hero) went into bat for both of us eventually telling the driver that if he didn't slow down he would need to stop and let us out. We made it home eventually and I couldn't have been more grateful to have had such a brilliant captain for that day - Kev is still a good friend and a good laugh and one of very few people who I could have flown an aircraft with, not wearing my trousers!!!

Now and again there would be a little gem waiting at the end of a seemingly big pile of dung. One day I am called from standby to take an empty aircraft to Paris Orly. This is not one of our usual airports and my captain is the same one who operated the private jet to Ajaccio. The weather in France is terrible - heavy snow showers have closed Orly and Charles De Gaulle - the two major airports for Paris - throughout the day and this has caused many delays and cancellations - which is why we need to take the spare aircraft there. We already know that we will be staying overnight but as is always the case in these situations, we don't know where yet. We make it safely to Orly, park up and head to the crew room to find out our fate for the evening.

A quick call back to Luton where crewing and operations are based, tells us that all hotels around Orly are fully booked and they are working as hard as they can to find us somewhere to stay for the night. Eventually, they call us back and say they are very sorry but the only hotel they can find for us is in Paris itself and because everything around the airport is in a state of complete chaos, they are unable to find us a taxi. If we are happy to arrange our own then they will reimburse us. No problem, we think, what's the name of the hotel? We scribble the details down on a piece of paper and go to try and find a taxi. The snow is thick, there are crowds of stranded passengers everywhere, and not a taxi or bus to be seen. That's about right! We know from experience that there is no point trying to get hold of anyone in Luton to try and sort this out for us because they will be up to their eyeballs trying to sort out all the other crew all over Europe who are now out of position, out of hours and need hotel accommodation.

We must have a guardian angel watching over us however, as one of the ground staff sees us in uniform and realises that although between us, our French is OK, it doesn't quite cut it for this situation - he comes to our aid, and within a few minutes has organised us a taxi from I don't know where! We are relieved when it arrives, and we are on our way to the hotel. We have no idea what this hotel will be like and joke on the way into the city that it is probably some awful low-budget place given the shortage of accommodation - but to be honest we don't care. If it has a bed, a shower and a bar we will be OK!

As we get further into the city we start to recognise some landmarks - this is looking remarkably familiar actually - and the only times I have been to Paris have been to visit the famous tourist spots right in the centre - which is where we are now, as our taxi pulls up alongside the Tuileries and stops at the Westin Paris Vendome - it is what we have written on our piece of paper so we decide to take our chances and find that yes, two rooms have been booked for us and it's all sorted. To say it is the poshest hotel I have ever stayed in would not quite be true - but it is up there in the posh hotel stakes and the price per room is eye-watering - it's a good job we are not having to pay for it!

By now it is after 11 pm and we have been on duty for far more hours than it would normally take to pick up a jet in Stansted and drop it off in Paris - it's not that long a flight after all - but as soon as any bad weather starts to disrupt things, everything moves at a snail's pace. We are not allowed to be on duty for 12 hours and have been booked onto the first flight home the next day that we are legally allowed to be on - it's at 4 pm so we have all day the next day if we want it.

That gives us plenty of time to decide that as it is coming up to Christmas, and it's not often you get to stay in the centre of one of the loveliest cities in the world at the company's expense, the decent thing to do is to go and find a bar which we do and settle down to a few beers and stories until well into the small hours.

The next day, the captain is supposed to be at birthday beers for a friend in London in the evening and doesn't want to miss it, so we decide to get an earlier flight home - this is something that we are allowed to do by choice, but the company is not allowed to make us do - there are a lot of protections in place like this and my company is very good at sticking to them. The earlier flight means that we need to be up reasonably early to get breakfast and head to the airport so in the end, we get to spend around 6 hours sleeping in this gorgeous and very expensive hotel, one which I suspect I am unlikely ever to have the opportunity to stay in again and especially in the run-up to Christmas. It is a shame because for just a few hours we got to taste the very rarely glamorous side of our jobs but as we board our flight back to the UK we are both glad to be on the downward slope towards our days off, London and home.

Chapter Six

Captain Mummy

Out of all my friends from school or University, I was the oddball - eleven days after I proudly graduated with a Bachelor of Arts with Honours in History from the University of Leeds, I found myself attending a ceremony of a different kind - with me very much in centre stage.

On what was to be the hottest day of the summer of 1995, I woke up in the Coach House of my parent's cottage, with my two bridesmaids ready to take on my wedding day. I was 22 years old and marrying the dashing RAF navigator I had met at RAF Finningley just 18 months earlier.

We wake up a bit bleary-eyed having drunk through my 'last night of freedom', and hilariously, my chief Bridesmaid Rona starts re-enacting the first scene of Four Weddings and a Funeral... we are in stitches and impressed at how completely hilarious we all are! Thankfully after a week that has been cold enough to prompt my parents to hire space heaters for the wedding reception, it is a clear and sunny day and at 8 am, already hot - far too hot in fact for us to be putting on posh dresses but that isn't until later. I am not in the slightest bit nervous. Today I am marrying a man I am completely in love with and since everyone else seems to like him too there is no pressure, no tight-lipped tolerance, in fact it is worse than that - I have already come to realise that my parents may like the man who is about to become my husband even more than they like me!!! (Note - writing this 28 years later, I am still married to the same man, and I can confirm that this is indeed the case - harrumph!)

The official story of how we met is that we were introduced in the Officers Mess bar at RAF Finningley - and this is true - Jim was the only one in the group who wasn't called something mad like Smash or Magoo or Turkey (these aren't the birth names of some of our friends but they do exist as real people!) - and we both found out at a later date that as I walked away from the group thinking, 'I'm going to marry that man one day.' He was also thinking, 'That's the girl I'm going to marry' - we are that cheesy. Our actual getting together was all down to a night out in the social Mecca that is Doncaster though, and anyone who was there in the 1990s will remember Charisma, the fact that it had almost none, and it was in this salubrious nightspot that handsome Jim sashayed (or staggered - we were quite drunk) onto the dance floor to, in his words, 'rescue me' and after the first dance, he asked me to marry him. He was messing around and so was I when I said yes, but only a bit!

So here we are on a hot summer day, in the garden of the house where I have lived for all but the first two years of my life, drinking Bucks Fizz in our pyjamas and doing a LOT of laughing. My dad is funny, for him, a day that passes without laughter is a day wasted and he sees and finds the funny side to everything - occasionally it's a bit much but mostly he is awesome, as is my very tolerant and very lovely mum. As parents they are chilled out about their oldest (and favourite obviously) child getting married at the age of 22 - a lot of parents would be fussing but they take everything in their stride, and we all know that this is going to be a good day.

Five hours later, having been to the hairdresser and managed to put some makeup on my normally naked face without making me look too much like Aunt Sally from Worzel Gummidge, everyone has left for the church, leaving only me and Dad at home - we decide that the only decent thing to do in this situation to stop our emotions catching up with us completely is have one last and very classy fag in the garden before the claret Rolls Royce owned by my dad's mate Dave, comes back to pick us up for the big moment. It is so hot by now that I can feel sweat running down the back of my very beautiful slub silk simple wedding dress and Dad is doing a brilliant job of trying to keep cool in his full top hat and tails.

I grew up in a Christian family and our lives revolved around a vibrant and lively church which has been our extended family since my parents moved to my hometown when they got married, because of that, and the fact that both of us have large actual families, our wedding is big. It is also a military wedding and there are a large number of men dressed up in uniform and carrying swords which turns out to be a showstopper as the church we are getting married in is on the High Street.

Finally, the Rolls arrived, and Dad and I climbed in trying desperately not to squash my train, for the short drive into town. We make jokes and laugh all the way, and on this occasion, I know it is to cover up the monumental fact that although this will always be home, it won't be mine from now on, and, when we return from honeymoon, I will be moving 600 miles north - but we don't want to think about that right now. As we turn onto the High Street we see that a small crowd has gathered outside the church which makes us giggle and I have to stop Dad from pretending he is the King and doing a royal wave. Three hundred people filled the church I had spent my childhood in, and it was pretty fantastic to see it so full of people I love. Even more amazing is that having signed the register, we walk down the aisle as Mr and Mrs, and out through the guard of honour that is holding their swords up for us whilst another of our friends pipes us out of the church. I giggle as one of our friends tells me as we pass him that he got arrested the night before - they have clearly had a good night and in later years I will find out that this was the biggest wedding the town had seen, with the police closing the road for a while - the only time this had been known to happen before was a huge gypsy funeral a few years earlier - how true any of that is remains a mystery but as we wheelspin out of the car park (yes, that happened - it was a gravel surface) and swoosh off to our reception ten minutes away, we are already sharing stories about the night before.

It is a day that goes down in our memories and those of our friends and families as one of the best weddings ever - well it would for us wouldn't it - with perfect weather, bagpipes to pipe us into the reception, a jazz band, and finally a Ceilidh before we are asked to leave to allow the older generation to go home - it is well past midnight and one of our friends performs a Highland Fling as we leave for our hotel. The torrential downpour that took place just as we sat down to eat has turned the bottom of my beautiful cream dress completely black, but this can't spoil the day any more than some of Jim's uni mates deciding to go for a naked swim in one of the lakes, or the knowledge that my Grandma was left behind at the church and almost didn't make the photos - and we fly to Mombasa the next day for our honeymoon which was perfect in every way apart from the fact that we didn't see a single lion during the safari part of the holiday! This is a first-world problem!

I make a bet with my dad in those moments before we leave for the church that I won't have children for at least five years - having only just graduated, the bet is for a fiver, and five years later when I am pregnant with my third child, I offer him the fiver which he graciously declines.

By now, we have been living on the Moray Firth for five years and concluded fairly quickly that this was as good a time as any to have children. This decision was reached in the same way that we have made all major decisions over the quarter of a century that we have been married - over a bottle of wine.

It is my birthday, and we are at a local hotel having dinner and talking about what I am going to do with myself. I don't mind my job, but it won't lead anywhere and in any case, the office I work in is moving to Inverness which is a much longer drive and now is crunch time. I have considered and decided against two opportunities which I will look back on and wonder why I wasn't braver. One is the chance to sail a leg of the Whitbread round the world yacht race. I have grown up sailing, raced at University and still know one end of a boat from the other, but I decide in the end that it is not fair on Jim for us to borrow the money I would need to take part, or to be away for that long - almost fifty-year-old me will look back on this moment and give me a stern talking too! The other is a British Airways cadetship which I applied for and have been accepted into. The training is at Prestwick, which is at least a four-hour drive away from home, and whilst fifty-year-old me will by now be shaking me and trying to get me out of this slightly trance-like state I surely must be in to turn down such an opportunity, 23-year-old me doesn't have things like the internet, or even a phone that is not attached to a wall - these are the days where there is only mail - you know, the kind that comes through the door in an actual envelope, is written by hand, with the address written on the front and not appearing on bank notepaper through a clear plastic window. These are the halcyon days of BT phone cards, reversing the charges, arranging to meet up with someone, and turning up on time and in the right place because there is no way of letting them know you are running late because you accidentally spent too much time on Facebook before you went in the shower - not just me surely?

So, if I am not going to go and sail around the world, and I am not going to train to be a pilot, what AM I going to do? Painting plant pots and making dough dollies (oh yes, I considered these as career possibilities) aren't going to cut it so I either need to re-train to do something useful, or... there is one other possibility.

"We could start a family," suggests Jim - we have reached desert by now in the stylishly fitted out Bistro part of the hotel, and the only other couple to dine that night have left already - I look at him to see if he is joking but he is deadly serious - we start giggling at the thought of us being parents when we are basically still children ourselves but decide that yes, this would be a great idea - and anyway it takes ages to have a baby doesn't it? We probably won't have children for several years... we are so giggly leaving the hotel to drive home that Jim is adamant that they will think we are both drunk. Little did we know that within the space of the next four years, we would have three very gorgeous (and a little bit naughty) children and our family would be complete by the time I was twenty-eight.

By the time I was pregnant with number three, it was a good job that my dad refused to take the £5 I offered him having lost the bet, because everyone knows that the best thing anyone can do when they are expecting a baby, is to decide to build a house - said no one ever, and so it is that when baby three is a week overdue, I find myself standing in the foundations of what will be our home, walking up and down behind a compactor which is pressing down all the sand into the foundations to prepare it for the concrete lorries which will need to come in over the next week. I am very fat (with child), very hot, and very bored of being pregnant. I just want to meet my baby and since it won't come out on its own, I think that this machine might even help to shake it out - not only that, we are on such a tight budget that there is no one else to do this work - the other two children are at nursery school and this is how I spend my days...

Finally, very suddenly, and with almost no warning, our third (and final) child screeches into the world, late but extremely chilled out, around 3 in the morning, and by lunchtime, I am at the builders merchants taking the compactor (which has done its job in more ways than one) back, before a trip to the "golden arches" to feed my bewildered bigger babies, the oldest of which is having to be bribed to believe that he has another sister and that no matter how much he wants it to happen, her name is not, and never will be baby Ovver (he can't say Oliver which is what she would have been if she had been a brother). She has brought him a toy train, and a baby doll for her big sister, and so far, so good.

These three tiny dots of awesomeness spend their lives hanging out at our building site, playing in the back of an old Land Rover my dad has bought to keep up here (knowing we will find it useful), making things out of building sand, and sometimes, getting to have a ride in 'daddy's digger', a thirty-year old JCB we have bought to help us with some of the work - I am convinced that this is more because it is fun to drive than because it is really useful but it does the job - apart from the time I arrive at the 'site' with some lunch for Jim with the kids in the car, only to find smoke pouring out of this prized possession of his, and start reversing quickly - there is no way I am taking my family near that mess, and as Jim runs towards me I reverse even faster thinking he wants me out of the way too - in actual fact he is chasing me because he knows there is a fire extinguisher in the car which he urgently needs and I watch in horror as he grabs it from the boot, puts the fire out and we gingerly assess the damage. It ends up needing a new engine, and somehow we laugh about this - I have been well-trained by Dad!

Eventually, the walls of the house go up (thanks to the dedication and commitment of the rugby team who turn up every Saturday morning at 8 to drive dumper trucks and mix cement and help us to build....), the roof goes on, we have windows, doors, ceilings and floors and although we are not in for Christmas, we move in February and start a new life in the house that everyone thought we were mad to build. The children have a mud garden to play in which they do with gusto, and since there are no walls or fences, they often wander out into the field and come back munching carrots which they have pulled out of the ground and eat unwashed. They are always grubby, always moving around, and everything they do makes a complete mess. I love it, and I am happy with my days being filled with finger painting and playdough, and my evenings being filled with plastering, painting and finishing off the inside of our home which was little more than a shell when we moved in.

It takes us a year to finish and we have decided that this is where we will stay. The RAF has other ideas however, and almost exactly a year after the day we moved in, we are in the business class lounge at Heathrow waiting to board an Air New Zealand Boeing 747 bound for Los Angeles where we will stop for three days before flying on to Auckland where we are to spend the next three and a half years on exchange. Those years on a military exchange on the other side of the world become a story in their own right, but I arrive as an overweight, drinking, smoking, sloth and leave as a slim, fit, triathlete, half marathon running commercial pilot thanks to a conversation with Jim a few months after we arrive.

We have settled very happily into a beautiful weatherboard house on the air base, the children have made friends, we are spending time with my brother and his family who have been there for several years, and for some reason, the idea of flying again comes onto our radar. A company called CTC has been advertising in the UK for people who want to learn to fly and end up in the right-hand seat of a passenger-carrying jet, and I apply to them asking if they would consider taking me on given that I am already in New Zealand. The answer is no but for the unexpected reason that at 30, I am too old. I am a bit shocked and more than a bit upset by this - how can I be too old to learn to fly? I question this with them asking them what reasoning they have for the cut-off age of twenty-seven. They have no good reason to give but the answer is still no. It feels so wrong that I am disqualified from this opportunity because of an age limitation. Within a year, age discrimination was banned but it was too late for me by then because Jim had already suggested that if I give up smoking, the money we save in UK pounds would pay in NZ dollars for a private pilot's licence - but there is a caveat. I have to give up smoking for six weeks before I can commit to flying. I think this is a fair deal but warn Jim that if I start flying again I probably won't stop and that could get expensive. Amazingly, he isn't worried about that part of it. We have always tended to cross bridges as we get to them, and this is no exception.

The incentive to stop smoking is even stronger when my dad ends up in Auckland Hospital with a DVT after flying out to see us - we decide to challenge each other to stop and the gauntlet is thrown down - this will be much harder for my dad in many ways as he has been smoking for a lot longer - but we decide to give it a go. I have one small problem though - I am already fat. I have had three babies in 3 1/2 years and am carrying a lot of extra weight which I have struggled to lose because as well as being busy looking after them and building a house, I am really lazy. I am one of the people at school who knew the shortcuts on the cross country run so I could pretend I wasn't unfit and have rarely run anywhere before. I notice that even running around with the children leaves me short of breath - this is not good. It is the kick up the arse that I need to do something about my lifestyle, and I decide that if I am not going to smoke any more, I need to take up sports to prevent myself from becoming even bigger. When I read an advert in a magazine for a 'Try a Tri' and the distances seem reasonable. A 300m swim followed by a 10k cycle and a 3k run. I can swim - that's a good thing - I have grown up swimming and love it, and I can ride a bike - another hangover from my youth - but running is my nemesis - I hate even the idea of it - but I think that I have nothing to lose from trying.

The first time I ran was in the evening when it was already dark. There is NO WAY I want anyone to see what I am doing. Everyone we know in Auckland is into sport of some kind, and it feels like most of them have competed at international level in one sport or another - the last thing I want is for anyone to see the fat English exchange wife plodding her way around an embarrassingly short course, out of breath, purple with effort, and being overtaken by a tortoise! The first day, I only manage to run as far as the end of the road which is not far at all, but I do it, and decide that I must keep doing it every day until I can run with some degree of, if not ease, then at least the ability to breath. Each day I run a little bit further and as I grow in confidence and tell my Kiwi friends what I am doing they couldn't be more supportive - in fact, they are amazing! They start to run with me, never minding the slow pace, and gradually, I build the distance up to the point where I can manage the whole 3km. It might not seem far to lots of people but to me, it is a really big deal. It also means that I have not smoked for long enough that I can start to fly, and so one day we take the plunge and walk over to the flying club on the air base and ask about lessons. I am assigned an instructor, Warren who not only gets me through my Private Pilot's Licence but along with Craig who does the same for my Commercial Licence, becomes a friend for life.

By the time we return to the UK, I am a commercial pilot and after completing the sixteen professional exams I must pass to fly for a UK airline, I land a scholarship to become a flying instructor. The very grand-sounding Guild of Air Pilots and Air Navigators offers me an interview and as part of this, I have to give a presentation. Having been advised against talking about anything to do with aviation on the basis that they will always

93

know more than me at this stage, I opt to talk to them about caffeine in food and drink, and the effect it has on our bodies. I take along samples of food and cans of drink that are loaded with caffeine and my 45-minute interview lasts 90 minutes at which point the interview panel is reminded that they have other people to see and could they please get on with it! I am awarded the Diamond Jubilee Scholarship which is presented to me in the Guildhall one autumn evening and start my training to teach other people to fly the following week.

By now we are living near High Wycombe where my husband works and to study for my exams I have been walking the children to school in the morning, coming home to walk the dog, and then shutting myself away in the study to make sure I know everything I need to know to pass. It is a juggling act. I only have 6 hours each day to do this, and as every mother will know, in that time I have to not only walk the dog but do all the other things that mums do every single day to make sure their household is clothed and fed, and more often than not, these things take more time than anyone plans for. Somehow, I manage to continue this when I am training too - that is far easier to fit into the day as it is a smaller window of time I need to allow, but when I am offered a job having passed my Flight Instructor course I have a dilemma. Do I ask the flying school if I can work school hours only? They are open to that but in return, I will be needed at weekends. The other option is to work from 9 to 5 and find childcare for two hours after school. We decide to look for an au pair, and after a false start with a girl who leaves after a month because she has accepted another job back at home, we welcome possibly the smiliest person I have ever met into our home to look after the children and help out. Jana is from the Czech Republic and arrives just before Christmas which she decides to spend with us as we are travelling to see my husband's family and she will see more of the country. By the time she had to leave the following summer, she had become an essential part of our family, but lots had changed for us too. I had been through an assessment to potentially fly for easyJet but had not yet heard if that will come to anything. We have also been posted back to Scotland and will be moving in the summer. We are excited to finally be going home and I managed to find a new job as an instructor on the base at Kinloss where we live.

I have landed on my feet once again and having worked for a training centre that was happy for me to take the summer holidays off initially, I find myself once again working for someone open to this too, although there are some Saturdays and evenings when I need to be at work. Having failed to attract an au pair to come and live with us in the north of Scotland, we manage to find a childminder to cover the two hours after school when I am working, but this is a constant worry as one has to leave for personal reasons, another becomes too ill to work, and the third ends up being posted away. Jim and I are constantly worrying about how we can manage to look after the children whilst still allowing me to work, and then I am offered a type rating course to join easyJet as a First Officer. I have mixed emotions about this. I am over the moon that I will now have the chance to join an airline, but equally, how can I leave my children and my husband behind? We have always been together, and it is Jim who does the going away, not me - being a RAF Officer he has been away so many times since the children were born that it is just a normal part of our lives. This has always been possible because although I have been working, I have always known what the children are supposed to be doing and when, and it seems almost impossible to think about leaving them behind and not knowing when I will see them again. I am so torn about whether or not this is the right thing to do that even the night before I am due to leave and drive south, I don't know if I can go through with it or not. I love these little people more than anything else in the world and I can't help wondering if this is such a completely selfish thing to do that I should pull myself together and stay at home to make sure they have the stability they will need as they grow older. I have been going round and round in circles about this, sometimes talking to friends who already have careers, who point out that if I were already working I wouldn't hesitate to be going back to work and that my children would be used to it. There are plenty of women who are mothers and have careers so it's not as if my children will be the first and only ones ever to have to understand that mummy can work too. I have plenty of girlfriends who are in the military, have children, and are deployed overseas from time to time, and to them, this is a no-brainer. The problem for me is that I have chosen to make my family my career, and I am effectively walking away from them to pursue something that is for me. I know that if I go through with this, it will start a chain of events that will change our lives forever, I don't know if I want that change - I have never relished the thought of things changing, I have coped with the constant moving around and never being able to guarantee Jim's attendance at weddings and birthdays but I don't love it.

The flip side of this is that I have also worked extremely hard over the last 6 years to reach this point. I have studied for and passed 33 professional exams between New Zealand and the UK to achieve the licence I now hold, not to mention invested a huge sum of money, hours and hours of time, and had the support of all of our parents and friends as well as the one person who has made all of this possible - Jim. How can I walk away from that?

Leaving my children behind on that day is one of the hardest things I have ever had to do, and I will never know what would have happened if I had made a different decision. It is also one of the bravest things I have ever done, and as the hours pass on the long drive south I start to think about the new life and new opportunities that will come our way if I am successful in passing this course. By the time I reach our friend's house in Marlow where I am staying for a night to break the journey, I am excited about what the future holds and have produced a plan to stay as connected as I possibly can to my children while I am away. I have already stopped and bought the children puppet kits which they can make and tell me about on the phone (the miracle of FaceTime is still a long way off) and every week I will send them something to remind them that I am still there.

Arriving at Botley Park Hotel and Golf Course the next day, I meet my course mates, all of whom are to become the kind of friends you never lose, and one of whom was to become a close friend. Simon is a flying instructor like me, has small children, and lives not far from my parents in Essex. We have lots in common and leaving our children behind becomes the thing that bonds us. Partway through the course, we are starting to get nervous about the lack of communication we are receiving about where we are likely to be based and when we will officially start working for easyJet. All of us need to know what is happening as we all need to make plans, but Simon and I also need to put childcare in place if we are going to be working in London. We decide to speak to one of the course directors and explain our position to him, we tell him that it doesn't matter too much if the answer isn't what we want to hear but that being told nothing at all is difficult and he promises to try and find some answers for us.

Three days later, he walks into the classroom and explains that whilst we will be finishing the course, there is not enough capacity in the training system at the airline to complete our training that summer and so once we have finished, we will be asked to go home and wait until there is an opportunity to finish our training. It is not the answer we wanted, but at least we know where we stand, and so having completed the course, we all drive home again, and back to the lives we thought we had left behind.

By now I have given up my instructing job at Kinloss and someone has already been employed to replace me. Someone must be watching over me however, as very soon after I return

GROUNDED

home, I am contacted by the flying club in Inverness and asked if I would be interested in becoming the deputy to the chief flying instructor. This is brilliant for many reasons, and once again I am in the happy position of being able to work around the children and take as much of the summer holidays as I need to. This is such a gift as I know more than ever that this might be the last summer I will get to spend with the children without any restrictions and although I work hard, I make sure I make the most of every single minute I have with these resilient and forgiving little people.

Shortly before Christmas, I get a call asking me if I could re-do the type rating starting on 3rd January - there is now some slack in the training system, and we are being recalled. There is no way that I can manage to organise childcare with three weeks' notice when one of those weeks is Christmas and the other is New Year - I am allocated a course later in January and although I know I need to go and get on with it, I still have a heavy heart at the thought of leaving the children behind, knowing that this time, it is going to be for at least the rest of their childhoods if not longer. From now on, our lives are going to revolve around both of us managing careers and it is going to be a steep learning curve once again I wonder if this is the right thing to do.

Ironically, the night before I am due to leave, heavy snow is forecast in the Highlands and even down to low levels. We live by the sea and rarely get snow that lies on the ground. I decide as I go to bed that night having spent longer than usual reading stories to my babies (they are hardly babies by now at 8, 10 and 11 but they are still young enough to need to know that I am

99

there) that if I am supposed to go and do this training, the roads will be open in the morning. If the roads are closed and I can't travel, that will be enough for me to know that it is not the right thing to happen.

I wake up early the next morning to see snow on the ground in our garden and I am almost hoping that the roads will all be blocked, and I can avoid the difficult path, and stay in my nice, safe bubble of domestic bliss, being the mummy I promised to be. The road we normally take runs over exposed moorland to pick up the A9 south and that is closed. The alternative route through Grantown on Spey is also closed, however, the road through to Inverness is open as is the A9 south - even over the Drumochter pass which is the highest point on the route. If Drumochter is open, I can try and get through so the decision is made. I hug my babies and Jim goodbye for what will be the last time for several weeks, get in our ancient Volvo, take one last look back at them standing there in their pyjamas and dressing gowns, holding their bears and blankets and trying not to cry, and drive away waving as tears roll down my cheeks that don't stop until I have to pull in to the petrol station just outside Inverness that has taken me an hour to reach instead of the usual 40 minutes. It is really cold and as I drive further south and further into the Cairngorms, all thoughts of my family are conveniently pushed to one side as I focus on following the narrow tracks in the snow that have been left by the car ahead of me. I have to stop every 30 minutes to scrape ice off the windscreen as the washer fluid is still frozen and going through Drumochter the temperature drops to minus

17C. I keep thinking that at some point the road will become completely impassable and I will turn around, drive home and sit in front of the fire with my family in the evening laughing at Mummy's funny idea that she was going to go away be an airline pilot, but by the time I reach the tourist Mecca that is the House of Bruar and stop for a cup of coffee, the snow has eased off, the roads are black and wet instead of brown and slippery and my way south is clear.

This time, some of my course mates are friends from the last type rating, but we are mixed in with a group of current easyJet pilots who are converting onto the Airbus from the Boeing 737. Having been stuck in traffic on the way to Southampton on the first morning I arrive fashionably late to be greeted warmly by Dave, our Ground school instructor who remembers me from last time and is a hoot. As I screech late into class giggling and apologising and saying hello to my friends from before I can feel the eyes of the rest of the room on me wondering who the hell just walked in and interrupted. Fortunately, they are a friendly lot and after my initial dodgy start, we all get on well. I am sitting next to a captain who also has three young children, and a wife named Emma, and we even have the same car - we also both like to talk, and we become good friends over the next few weeks. One day we are talking about where my career might go, and I tell Rob that I would like to fly long haul. "You don't want to do that," he says, "imagine being stuck down route one day when little Johnny falls out of a tree and breaks his leg, you would hate it." I have never thought about it like that before and this is the first time that the advantage of working for an airline that comes back to base every night sinks in.

My sim partner from the previous type rating has not returned as his wife has recently had a baby, and I am paired up with a really lovely young lad called John. We get on well and he becomes very protective of me later on in the course.

We are all staying in the same lovely hotel as before, and very early one morning, the phone in my room rings. This is completely disorientating because no one apart from my parents and husband has the number, and everyone knows that no one ever phones a landline with good news before 8 am. My mum is on the end of the phone which is also unusual. "Darling it's Mum, I'm so sorry to call you so early but something has happened." My heart almost stops, is it Dad, or Jim, or one of the children - why is Mum ringing me if it's them... "Andrew has had an accident, we don't know if he is going to make it, do you know how I can get to New Zealand today?"… shit... my brother, my only sibling - what does she mean about him not making it? She gives me the details of what's happened, and I tell her I will see what I can do - I haven't even started working for an airline yet but I do have a lot of friends who fly in New Zealand where my brother has lived for the last fifteen years. It turns out he was on his motorbike going to Kempo his martial arts class, and he came off on a corner. He has been found hanging over a tree down a ravine and airlifted to the local hospital where he is fighting for his life. My little brother, who is a six-foot-four strapping policeman - how can he be that seriously injured?

I make some calls, find out about the amazing compassionate fare that AirNZ operate, call Mum back and get her to book the next flight to Auckland. I arrange to meet her and Dad at Heathrow later that day which is thankfully a day off and wait until a decent time to call Jim. I have no idea what will happen now and all we can do is wait. I am too devastated to go to the dining room for breakfast - I can't look at people - so I order room service and text John who comes around straight away. He is amazing, and a complete rock, and what I don't know until later is that he goes to reception after he has seen me and asks them to divert any calls or visitors to him so that I am not disturbed. As the news spreads through the course and to our friends and family, the messages of support are overwhelming, and I wonder what my next move will need to be. I want to be with my family, but they are at the other end of the country and when I get to Heathrow to meet Mum and Dad we are all too stunned to even cry. There is still no news and as we send Mum on her way through security, I am so worried for her having to travel all that way not knowing if her son will still be alive when she gets there. Dad is going in a couple of days, and I worry about him driving home. We sit in a bar at the airport for hours after Mum has left talking about anything other than Andrew dying, and when we finally leave I make him promise to phone me as soon as he is safely home. I go back to the hotel via the training centre and speak to one of the nice people in the office to tell them what has happened. I don't know if I need to leave the course or stick it out or what is going to happen, so they tell me to keep them posted as I am not due in the sim for another couple of days. The next 24 hours pass agonisingly slowly as Mum arrives in Hong Kong to find that there is no news, and then finally in Auckland where we have arranged for friends to pick her up and take her to my brother. He is alive, just, but he is in a bad state, and we still don't know if he will come out of the coma he is in, and if he does, what sort of recovery he can expect to make. Ridiculously, his bike has barely a scratch on it, and we find out that it is only thanks to a truck that was behind him and had noticed that he was no longer ahead of them and gone back to look for him along the road that he is even here at all.

I speak to Dad, and we agree that I should stay in the UK, since there is nothing that I can do to help anyone at the moment, the best thing is to throw myself back into my type rating. I speak to the training centre, and they are completely amazing - understanding immediately when I tell them what has happened, that I would like to carry on with the type rating, and that although I think the sim instructor should know what has happened I don't want to talk about it at all. I can't. The only way I can even keep breathing at the moment is to focus on what I have to do rather than on what might happen to my brother, and when I am in the sim, I switch off completely from what is happening in my world and smash out three of the best sim sessions I have probably ever had. It helps to spend four hours at a time completely immersed in something different, and I will always be so grateful to that wonderful and completely empathetic instructor who couldn't have been better placed to train me. He tells me that he had lost his wife during his first type rating and that his second wife is now in a wheelchair, so he completely understands why I want to continue with my training as a way of switching off.

John is also fantastic, and we sail through the rest of the sim sessions together, and now know where we are to be working. I have requested Stansted as it is close to my parent's house, and this is where I will be based. Simon is also going to be based at Stansted along with two others we have got on well with on the course - Graham and Craig. As proof that there are only six degrees of separation, Craig turns out to be the cousin of one of my oldest friends from home. Staying and completing the course was the right decision, as my brother has pulled through and although he is badly broken, he is alive. He is so badly injured that we don't know yet what the rest of his life will look like, but he is alive, Mum and Dad are with him, and because I am staying with them when I am working anyway, I am looking after their house. All is as well as it can be.

It is time to go home and spend some time with my family and I take advantage of the gap in training between finishing the type rating and starting the easyJet induction to go back home to Scotland and see how everyone is getting on without me. They haven't missed me at all - well not in a weeping and wailing kind of way, and Jim has done an amazing job of being mummy and daddy to the children while I have been gone - in fact, he tells me it's been really easy and he doesn't know what all the fuss has been about when he has been away - my response to that is not printable!

Now that I have started working, we need to find a more permanent solution to who is going to look after the children when I am not here. We also need to find a more stable way of educating them - they have been in three different education systems in three different countries by now and I am worried that things are being missed. Our son has started at our local prep school and the girls seem keen on it too. I have always been adamant that my children will not go to boarding school - it was not how I did education and no one else was going to bring my children up. Life doesn't always work out like that though does it, and sometimes we have to change our ideals to suit the situations we either find ourselves in or create. In our case, the trade-off for me working is that I need to change my views on boarding school and since the one we have chosen for our children is only down the road from our home, it is a no-brainer. We can only do this with the help of the RAF however, and this is known as golden handcuffs because signing up to receive continuity of education allowance (CEA) means that you must accept postings to wherever they want to send you. We think long and hard about keeping our youngest daughter at home with us, but she is fiercely independent even at nine and insists that she wants to be wherever her brother and sister are. Her age makes this a really tough call. She is old enough not to want to be treated like a baby, but still young enough to have long bedtime stories, and she is also our baby - we have long talks about what is the best thing to do but in the end boarding school wins. Jim is from a military family and he and his cousins all went to boarding school and loved it - and anyway, we would only be down the road - or so we thought. The girls joined our son at prep school with the promise that daddy would be unlikely to be posted away and that they would soon be able to be day pupils in line with the rules at the time. They are happy with this and although I am not ecstatic at the thought of them being sent away to school, I can tolerate it because it is not too far away. In the autumn, there is a strategic defence review and the new maritime patrol aircraft my husband has been working so hard to help deliver, the Nimrod MRA4 is about to be signed off to enter service. He comes home from work one day frustrated that there has been another delay to the paperwork saying, "I just don't understand why they don't just sign the airworthiness certificate and release it to service." The Nimrod is why we are here, and we are confident that despite the occasional posting somewhere else, Jim can pretty much see out the rest of his career here.

I arrive at work early one day when I get a call from Jim, "They've chopped it," he says. "What are you talking about?" I reply. "They've cut the bloody Nimrod, they are scrapping it, Kinloss is closing." I am too stunned to know what to say next. How can an island nation just scrap its maritime defence aircraft? It doesn't make any sense at all, but it is what has been decided and within days, there are images on the news of the recently converted aircraft, along with all but two or three of the original Nimrods being destroyed by diggers. A shockwave ripples through our corner of the RAF. We have spent 15 years of our lives associated with this air base and planned our future here, and now the aircraft and the base that supported it are gone. The only way that Jim can keep his job is for him to accept a posting south. This is what we signed up to and agreed when we accepted the boarding school 'golden handcuffs' and it is what we must do - but it means moving south and leaving the children as full-time boarders or pulling them out of school and taking them with us as we bounce around what is left of the RAF. It is a bleak prospect and once again I find myself grateful for having a job that requires my full attention as it leaves no room for navel-gazing and we must just get on with it.

We give the children the choice and they choose to stay where they are. We will keep our house and stay in it whenever we come to visit but otherwise, we will now be living in Buckinghamshire for the second time - but this time further north near Aylesbury. I drive over to visit our new home one day with my mum and have to admit that although it is not the beautiful home that we have built and which is stuck together with our blood sweat and tears, it looks ok and is in a nice area, and crucially, close enough to Stansted for me to be able to drive to work every day.

It is very weird moving for the first time, to a new place, without your children when you are used to having them around. There is no school gate to meet new friends at, no after-school clubs or parents of friends to get to know, and a clean and tidy house is no compensation at all for not having the people you love most in the world around you. There is an upside which is that you can do whatever you want, whenever you want, but on balance, I prefer to have the children close by. We move in January. I fly to London to start my block of work leaving Jim to supervise the removals and drive south with the dog. We promise the children we will be back to see them in three weeks and already have flights booked. On moving day, I operate an early Amsterdam and having left mum and dads with a car full of all the rubbish I seem to accumulate wherever I lay my hat, I drive straight to our new house arriving in the middle of the morning, which is just in time to make the removal men a cup of tea. The secret to a great move is to keep the people who are sent to move you fed and watered at all times, and always thank them with beer. This is how we have got through six moves so far in fifteen years which is not many compared to some military families.

It is a filthy January day, pouring with rain and everything gets covered in mud as we all squelch from the lorry to the house, I decide to escape to the relative safety and calm of John Lewis where I bulk buy enough sets of curtains to cover at least the windows we have to look at to make it feel more like home.

This is the new pattern for the next 7 years of our lives. I can drive to work, and come home every night, at least one of us visits the children every 3 weeks, they fly down for holidays and long weekends, and although we initially keep our house just for us to use, we eventually decide to rent it out as a holiday let when we are not using it to help it pay some of the bills. Although it is not what we had imagined all those years ago on the night we decided to start a family, we are happy and we manage to keep everyone together, making the most of living near London, and near an airport to take the children on trips to Iceland, Croatia,

Barcelona, Paris and anywhere we feel like going. Our house in Scotland will always be home but we make the best of everywhere we live in between.

As the children get older they can fly unaccompanied and although it never gets any easier to say goodbye to them, we find ways of making the long-distance relationship we now have with our children work. In this way, we are no different from the hundreds of military families who do this every year, and I gradually accept that sending the children to boarding school is the best way of providing them with a stable education, whilst also knowing that they are in a safe place and being looked after, and it is typical that having decided to send them to a local boarding school, we end up moving back to our house in Scotland just as they are leaving school and heading out into the world. We have managed, with a lot of juggling to keep balls in the air, to combine two careers with seeing the children at every opportunity, and somehow not only stayed married through it all but also mostly sane.

We had some tricky moments, like the time I took a call from Jim during a turnaround at Stansted telling me that he was deploying and would be gone by the time I got home. He had been on three hours' notice to leave, and I wasn't allowed to know where he was going or how long he would be away. My mum was on her way over, so I wasn't to worry. The children were understandably upset but Mum would arrive before he left. The call ended with him saying "I will speak to you whenever I can and I love you", and then he was gone. Another time I had to phone my boss to explain that thanks to another short notice posting, I was the only person who could deliver the children back to school after the summer holidays and could I please have compassionate leave? My boss had children who were a similar age and was thankfully very understanding. He also knew that during term time I would go wherever and whenever I was needed to help my colleagues out so there was plenty of payback.

We have had to make decisions that we never wanted to have to make when it has come to being parents and juggling careers, but the amazing adult children we have now are not only a testament to the fact that this can be done but also prove that it is possible to maintain a close family unit despite large distances, sudden deployments, several house moves and all the topsy turvy bits and pieces that have made up the tapestry of our lives, and we are grateful for every single moment.

Chapter Seven

Inside the Cockpit - or "Mother Theresa Meets The Red Baron"

WhatsApp Message

> Morning Em... I have just been asked to suggest names for another season of documentary - they want some grown ups this time - are you in?

> Errr... sure, as long as they don't make me look like an idiot - I can do that all by myself lol!

In 2017, easyJet had agreed to allow cameras into the flight deck and onboard flights in order to 'bring the flight deck to the people' and show what happens during the course of a working day.

There were some good bits - but on the whole, it was a bit of a disaster and painted a view of aircrew that was untrue, unprofessional and brought disrepute onto our industry. It was not well received by those of us who work hard to show the professional but also human side of the industry, and it also didn't go down well with the public - it definitely wasn't what the airline had hoped for either. In fact, it was so bad that the third episode was never aired and only appeared online.

I remember thinking, 'thank goodness that didn't involve me.' My brother in law is a BAFTA nominated TV producer and director and his words of wisdom when our children's school featured in a documentary was, 'if you see cameras, run in the other direction because you will never have any control over anything that is used - and they will always find an angle.'

So in 2018, when I received this message from my good friend Zoe (who had appeared in Season one and come across brilliantly - because she is - well, brilliant), I had to have a bit of a think about whether or not I was willing to expose myself to this kind of scrutiny, knowing that I wouldn't have any control over how that would be edited and what the reaction of my colleagues and friends would be.

My decision was that I would meet with the editorial team and find out what they were aiming to achieve this time, and also to lay down some ground rules around what would, and wouldn't be OK for me if they wanted me to participate.

We met on a grey afternoon at Starbucks (other coffee shops are available) in Gatwick's North Terminal and I admit I was quite excited about what they were looking to do.

"We know the last series wasn't great, and we really want to have another opportunity to show the airline and your profession in a better light - show it like it is."

I could get on board with this. Since gaining my command a

couple of years earlier, I had gone to great lengths to establish my own style of being a captain. Leading my crew from the front as it were - but also making sure I was really visible to passengers. I knew from the work I was doing as one of the airlines Fearless Flyer presenters, that 20% of my passengers were in some way uncomfortable about what they were about to do, and that seeing my face, and being told what was happening in the event of a delay, could help with this. I felt there would be an opportunity to actually show what it is like to work for a busy airline, in one of the most amazing 'offices' in the world, and that I could manage not to let myself down by saying or doing anything embarrassing.

There was another element to this though - my husband is an Officer in the Royal Air Force - and there was no way I was going to agree to anything that would bring him into disrepute either.

The next question was, 'Would you be willing to take part in this?" I said, "Yes, but I do have one or two stipulations. I will agree to participate as long as it doesn't bring me, the airline, my family or the RAF into disrepute in any way."

"We don't have to use you," was the reply.

"Absolutely you don't, but if you do, those are my terms."

I didn't hear any more about this until a few days later when I arrived at my aircraft to find a film crew fitting cameras to the top of the cowling where all the knobs and buttons are that we use to control the aircrafts direction, speed and altitude when the autopilot is engaged.

'I guess they agreed to my conditions then,' I thought, chuckling as I went through the pre-flight checks that must be carried out whenever you are about to operate your first flight of the day.

As a crew, we had briefed in the crew room in Gatwick's Jubilee House and this was not a normal flight. It was one of our Fearless Flyer flights. On this day, I was the operating crew, but on some days when we did this, I would give a 45 minute scripted presentation to around 300 nervous passengers and their companions before joining them on board a one hour flight which I would then narrate explaining all the noises, movements and sensations that were completely normal to me, but terrifying to some of our passengers because they weren't used to them.

It was a pretty standard UK wintry day - grey skies, chilly, but not raining and not windy which was great for our passengers as there was very little chance of turbulence.

My co-pilot, Josh, had received an email asking if he would be willing to be filmed as had the crew - I actually hadn't but I assumed that was because I had already had the conversation a few days before.

It was quite exciting knowing that we were going to be able to show people what happens in our world because as a child, I would go and visit the pilots on the flight deck on every flight I was lucky enough to be on. I grew up in the 1970s and 1980s, and we didn't fly nearly so often then. When we did, it was a big deal, and the biggest difference between then and now is that the flight deck door was always open - in fact, I don't even know if there WAS a flight deck door - or if these were retro-fitted after 9/11. There was a curtain to give the pilots some privacy while they were eating, but most of the time, if you asked nicely, you could wander up to the flight deck, say hello, have a look around, and see what was going on.

They were special moments for me. At every opportunity I would go and have a peep into this magical world at the front of the plane wondering if I would ever get to sit in that seat and be the Captain.

This was my chance to do the same through the medium of TV.

Our cameraman, Patrick, explained how it would all work. The camera rig had one camera pointing at each of our faces, and a fish eye camera filming us from the front, whilst a Go-Pro mounted to the jumpseat behind us would capture the flight deck and the view outside.

Of course, none of this could just be fitted randomly. It had all been approved and tested by our engineers and our operations department, and there was a special dispensation for this to be allowed to happen.

The film crew were not allowed to sit with us in the flight deck so they would be in the front row of the cabin with an iPad which would allow them to see what was happening, and to hear us at all times. We also had to have a separate microphone to be able to capture our voices since the flight deck is such a noisy environment, we mostly wear noise cancelling headsets.

They also explained to us that although we wouldn't have control over the final edit, there WAS a degree of control over what we would allow to be used - so that in the event of an emergency or something going wrong, we could ask them to delete the footage and they would do as we asked.

I was happy. It was a brilliant opportunity to invite people to see our world - and that was exciting, but we also had a job to do.

Josh and I decided that it would be best to act as if the cameras weren't there and behave as we normally would. That is exactly what we did. I didn't worry about saying the wrong thing or doing anything differently because cameras were there, and this turned out to be TV gold (I was later informed by the film crew).

This first flight only lasted an hour because it was Gatwick to Gatwick and specifically for the Fearless Flyer team to do their job, however, after that day, I had a film crew with me almost all the time, and on most of my flights.

I loved every second of it. I got to know Patrick (who I started to think of as 'my' cameraman) quite well - in fact we are still in contact from time to time - and I became known as 'one take Henderson' because whenever I was asked a question, I just answered it honestly and without hesitation.

I became so comfortable with the crew that they even came to my house very early one morning to film me having my breakfast before an early morning departure from Inverness. My husband was asleep upstairs, and stayed there while even the dogs behaved themselves.

Initially, my flights were quite run of the mill as they so often are - not very interesting footage, but on the morning we were filming from Inverness, I arrived at the aircraft to find a fault with one of the flight control systems. It was a fault I couldn't clear myself and I couldn't get airborne with, so there was no choice but to call the engineer out from his bed to come and fix it. This all took time, and so of course there was a lot to manage. Firstly arranging the engineer which was quicker for me than for our Ops department. Inverness is my 'home' airport and over the years I had got to know the staff there well. I had the engineers number in my phone so I called him and asked him to come and help - his name was Pavle and I was impressed at how quickly he arrived given he was asleep and had to drive to the airport, go through security and get out to the aircraft.

The fault was dealt with pretty quickly - an Airbus is an amazing machine with hundreds of onboard computers, circuit breakers, switches and relays, and more often than not, a fault can be fixed with a quick reset, or as anyone with a computer will know, switch it off and on again and it should sort itself out. Despite the ease of fixing these things however, given the extra dimension we work in every time we fly, it is essential that resets are signed off by a qualified engineer.

Despite acting as quickly as possible, there is an inevitable delay and once I have finished doing everything I must do in the flight deck, I head into the cabin to find out how our passengers are getting on. I have been giving regular updates on what time we can expect to arrive in London, and since it is such an early morning, a lot of people are dozing, but some are excited to see the cameras on board, and this is great footage for the film crew as they tell me.

A few days later, the crew are with me again as I fly to Pisa from Gatwick. This is what we call a three sector day and once again it will finish in Inverness.

Having got used to having the crew on board I just worked around them as we each go about our business.

The flight to Pisa is uneventful, but when we are boarding the return passengers I can hear something happening at the front of the cabin. I am in the middle of some paperwork but once I finish that off, the Senior Cabin Crew comes in and asks me if I can help by speaking to one of the passengers who is very nervous.

I arrive in the cabin to see a lot of fuss being made in the front row over a lady who is very distressed. She is a nervous flyer and through translators she tells me that she didn't want to fly but her friends had put a lot of pressure on her to take this trip and she didn't want to let them down - but now she is terrified and starting to feel unwell. I take her outside for some fresh air and reassure her that everything will be fine, also explaining to her that it is her choice to travel and not theirs. She calms down a little and we return to the front row where she starts to panic again.

She is still standing up when her legs buckle underneath her and she faints literally into my arms. I am reasonably strong but the deadweight of even this slim lady is quite a lot to manage. I am able to manoeuvre her into a seat and realise she is retching as I grab a sick bag for her. I am grateful there was one available when I feel the vomit hit my hand through the bag - and then I realise the cameras are still rolling - I tell them to stop filming as capturing this moment feels undignified. They stop filming immediately but they have all the footage they need and decide on the way home that they won't come to Inverness because they now have a story they can use.

Overall, 4000 hours are filmed of me and my colleagues at work, and all this has to be edited to produce three 45 minute episodes.

There are lots of moments they could use but I won't know until the series is released how much they will use of me, and crucially, how I will be portrayed.

There is one flight that I know will end up in the documentary and it is one of the most amazing moments of my flying career.

Towards the end of February I am operating to Keflavik in Iceland. It is one of my favourite destinations because it can be more challenging than some places we go to, it feels much further away than anywhere else, and in winter especially, there is always the chance of seeing the Aurora Borealis - the northern lights.

I see them regularly from my house in Scotland, but they are always low on the horizon and not always clear to the eye except through a camera; I use an app to tell me when there is a high chance of them being visible. On this day there is a very strong chance of seeing them, and so I ask permission from our Chief Pilot to take my DSLR camera with me in the flight deck. I wouldn't normally do this, but with the cameras on board, I want to make sure I have some top cover!

On the way up to Keflavik I realise with disappointment that my camera has been left switched on and has no battery left. I am gutted but there is nothing I can do about it.

When all our passengers are onboard, I stand at the front of the cabin as I usually do, to welcome them. I explain to them that there is a chance that we might get an Aurora display, and what we will do to help them to see it if this happens. I also explain that because I have told them of the possibility, it probably won't happen, and then tell them about the useless camera - which means it almost certainly will - they all laugh and there is excitement among most of the passengers who have spent a few days in Iceland with total cloud cover and not seen any Aurora activity.

We take off into cloud, and as we are climbing through 22,000ft I see a small glow in the distance. I point it out to co-pilot Greg wondering if I am imagining it. At first he can't see anything and I still can't tell, but then, suddenly, there it is - the glow gets bigger and brighter, and suddenly it explodes into a display of all the colours from green to red to yellow and purples and pinks. It is incredible.

We have reached our cruising altitude now and I speak to the Senior to let them know what we can see - we have pre-arranged that if there is something to see out of the windows, they will dim all the cabin lights so that everyone can see the display.

I make an announcement to the passengers and later on, I find out that everyone was very excited to finally get to see the Aurora that had eluded them on their trip.

I manage to take a few photos on my phone but they are quite grainy and can't do justice at all to what we are witnessing - it is disappointing but just being able to see it at all, and especially whilst at work, is incredible.

When we see the recorded footage from the Go-Pro in the

flight deck, it is amazing and as we are saying goodbye to our passengers back at Gatwick, one lady stops and tells me how grateful she is that they got to see the Aurora when she had thought it wouldn't happen. She was a professional photographer and had taken some amazing shots which she offered to email to me. I was so delighted to get a memento of that flight and still treasure this photo.

By the time the first episode of our series airs in May, I know that I feature quite a lot, but I don't know any of the content. The airline has advised us to shut down our social media accounts and not to look at comments or engage with any negativity, and my brother in law Mark has offered to keep an eye on it all for me.

I sit at home, on a night stop that evening, with a cushion ready to hide behind if it is really awful.

The programme starts, and the first three minutes are of me - I instantly get a text from Mark, 'This is huge! The first three minutes are what make people decide if they are going to watch or not - and they are all of you!'

As the programme continues, my phone starts to light up - so many people send messages saying how much they are enjoying watching, how much they love seeing me at work, and how good they think it is. I haven't had to hide behind the cushion once so far, and although I don't like the sound of my own voice - something my children especially will disagree with - I think it has gone ok.

Thanks to the narration of the legend that is Stephen Fry, I have just become known as Captain Emma, or more specifically on social media, #CaptainEmma. Apparently I am trending on Twitter and the comments are mostly nice.

There are one or two comments about whether or not I ever brush my hair, or stop eating - because both of those things profoundly affect my ability to operate a multi-million dollar passenger jet right - but on the whole, everyone is very positive - and I am hugely relieved.

Mark sends me screenshots of some of the best comments and they really are amazing!

Paul @p..........
We shouldn't give up hope. I'm sure if we campaign enough @emseyflyer will be on our screens again soon @itv are you listening!!!!!!!!!!!!!!!!

Fairylight @s..........
Replying to @pipp83_alt @emseyfler and 2 others. Yes I hate flying but she makes me feel that it would all be ok!!!

JanetB @J..........
@emseyflyer @easyJet never seen a
more positive and genuinely sincere
person, you're a credit to EasyJet

Amanda Jones @a..........
Captain Emma has such a positive way
of handling things & is great with the
passengers #insidethecockpit @easyJet

There were hundreds of messages like this and some of them were genuinely hilarious. In fact, they were so funny, and there was so much love, that Mark decided to turn all the screenshots into a gift for my husbands birthday.

Two personalised handkerchiefs arrived in the post so that Jim could forever blow his nose into nice comments that were made about me by people I didn't know.

Of all the comments, my favourite was this - and if you are out there somewhere reading this book @HumphreyGrizzle, I would like to thank you for creating the nickname that has stuck with my children ever since.

Sir Humphrey Grizzle @H.........
"My name is Emma I am your captain"
Whoa - female pilot!! Triple JD and coke please
steward. Think again. What a legend Captain
Emma is. Mother Theresa meets the Red Baron
and joins @easyJet. #insidethecockpit

My children thought this was SO hilarious that my name on all of our family group chats has ever since been 'Mother Theresa meets the Red Baron' and although they gave me a healthy dose of mickey taking which has kept me firmly Grounded (see what I did there!), I think they are secretly quite proud of what I do, and also relieved that I didn't embarrass them.

A few days after the show first aired, I was at the children's school where, each year, they hold a Highland Games. The phone rang and it was Johan Lundgren, CEO of easyJet.

He wanted to pick up the phone to tell me himself that he had been having dinner with some friends the night before, and they had all watched the show - he wanted me to know how much he and they had all enjoyed it and how delighted he was with the way everything had come across.

I had achieved what I had set out to achieve. I had been part of showing people a little window into the strange world we inhabit at 37,000 feet, with everything it throws at us. Drunk passengers, turbulence, fainting, delays, weather, early morning starts, late night finishes, fast-paced decision making, vomiting passengers, aircraft swaps, short notice changes, a different crew every day speaking 64 different languages and managing to do the same job in all those different conditions while delivering a safe outcome. That is what we are there to do - and it was an amazing privilege to have been able to show that to people who normally don't get to see the world from the pointy end of a plane.

The documentary also did something else for me that I wouldn't appreciate until several months later. It propelled me into a limelight I was comfortable in, and meant that I was well known not only throughout my own airline, but in many of the other airlines UK wide - and unknown to all of us at the time, this would give me a loud voice to go on and do something even bigger.

For now though, I was happy to revel in the success of the programme that I had been determined not to allow to be a disaster on my account - although if I do ever meet Stephen Fry - and I very much hope I do - I would like to have a word with him about him letting people think that I got lost in Amsterdam! If you know, you know, if you don't know, watch the episode and you will see - later in this book, I will explain what really happened! (Clue: it wasn't nearly as sensational as it was made to look!)

Chapter Eight

Grounded for a Higher Cause - Project Wingman

It is March 2020, and the country has just been placed into lockdown due to a virus that no one understands. Rumours are doing the usual rounds and whilst some people think it's all over, some believe it will all be back to normal in a couple of weeks, and most are just bemused. Jim is one of those who still thinks it will all be back to normal soon and is still going to work despite me asking him repeatedly not to. He has autoimmune diabetes and is therefore vulnerable and it is not until he hears a Radio 2 doctor talking about the risks that he starts to take things seriously and turns the car around on the way to work and returns home where he stays for the next two months. In the meantime, I have been talking to my friend and colleague Rob who I know through being a peer support mentor for my airline. Peer support is now an EASA-mandated requirement for all airlines thanks to the horrific German Wings crash in 2016, and I was one of the original peers who were trained to support our colleagues. This is how I got to know Rob and his colleague Adrian. Part of the training we undertook involved some role play and I immediately put my hand up to take part in a fake phone call in front of the other peers with Rob. I was playing the part of the person who needed help and Rob was the peer and by the end of the conversation, both he and I and the rest of the peers were falling around with laughter as the issues I brought into the conversation became more and more outlandish. I had invented an affair which I couldn't discuss with my partner and when he asked me why I explained it was with my boss. When pushed as to why this was such a problem I made sure I worded it so that it was clear that the affair was actually with the female CEO at the time, and this was the source of everyone's mirth. Rob and I found a connection on that day and had got to know each other reasonably well over the subsequent years and as I became increasingly frustrated at the thought of sitting on the ground doing nothing potentially for months, I decided to speak to him about an idea I have to try and help a national health service that we are all being told is becoming overwhelmed.

It turns out that he has been having a similar conversation with a Captain - Dave - from another airline and he connects us to talk about our ideas. We quickly establish that whilst he has the initial hospital contacts, I can put the word out and see who else wants to help and within a couple of days our 'back of the fag packet' plan is put into action with me setting up a Gmail account which we initially call 'nhsaircrewresponse' as we don't know what else to call it yet. The idea we come up with is a simple one. We will approach a London hospital local to Dave and ask them if they would like us to help them by providing some well-being support during the onslaught of what has become widely known as COVID-19. If the hospital agrees to provide us with a room that is large enough to practice social distancing, as well as some basic drinks and biscuits, we will provide a small team of aircrew to provide well-being support in the same way that we are used to caring for people on board our aircraft. The crew will be in uniform so that they are easily recognisable, and we realise that we need to come up with a suitable name for our little project. It takes nanoseconds for us to decide that the obvious choice is Wingman because we are offering to be 'Wingmen' to the NHS and any pilot that tells you they don't love Top Gun (even secretly) is telling fibs! We even decide which characters we are - although this is completely in jest and none of us wants to be known as Maverick anyway!

In the meantime, I spam every social media network I possibly can from the workplace to Facebook to LinkedIn and anything else I can think of, asking people to spread the word and sign up using the email address. In three days, seven hundred people have replied, and I can't manage to transfer all the details onto a spreadsheet on my own anymore, so I call Esther, a friend from my instructing days at High Wycombe and ask her if she fancies helping out. She jumps at the chance - Esther has already lost her job when UK regional airline FlyBe collapsed just before Christmas and has been left feeling a bit bereft. Not only does she get her teeth stuck into the job quickly, but she also makes a much better job of it than me (one of my few gifts is the ability to know when I am not very good at something and spreadsheets are just something that I don't really understand or ever feel the need to) - one thing I can do is design a logo and once this is done we use it on everything.

In these same three days, Dave has been writing manuals

for Hospitals and Volunteers as well as a risk assessment and is making some progress with two hospitals in London. The Whittington where his girlfriend works and The Royal Free where Rob works as a consultant psychologist. Rob is hoping the Royal Free will be the first one to take on this idea but in the end, it is the Whittington that becomes our Flagship lounge and three weeks after we have our initial conversation, we open the Wingman Lounge there with a Press Release managed by the hospital.

There are so many obstacles to overcome all the time that we find ourselves working all day, every day, late into the night, and also at weekends - it is relentless, but I am adamant that everyone who contacts us should get an answer, and we should always make ourselves accessible and contactable. We need publicity to get the word out to as many crew as possible that this is something they could sign up for if they are interested and also, to encourage more hospital trusts to take our idea on board. Covid may be the travel industry's nemesis, but it has opened doors and removed the red tape for us and our idea and once the Whittington has launched, it is quickly followed by trust after trust contacting us and asking us for help.

We realise that we need to produce some basic ground rules and probably more of a formal organisational structure and we now have six key players who are keen to keep things moving. Dave, Rob and myself as the founders have been joined by Alex who has volunteered to be Team Lead at the Whittington, Rich who is also supporting the Whittington and who is a colleague from my airline, and a friend of his called Tony who has experience of setting up and running charities and has offered to help us with this process and governance which we have no experience of at all. Together the six of us agree that we will set up a company called the Project Wingman Foundation Ltd and that we will also apply for charitable status. This means lots of meetings where we discuss our charitable mission and various other things, and I enlist the help of my local MP Douglas Ross to endorse our quest for charitable status in an attempt to get it granted quickly. I had been in contact with Douglas the previous summer to ask him to intervene in an industrial dispute between Air Traffic Control and Highlands and Islands Airports Ltd over pay which had resulted in a work to rule on the part of ATC. I am not disputing the rights and wrongs of this, but it was having an adverse effect on the people of the northeast of Scotland and their connectivity to London which so many people rely so heavily on for work, not to mention damaging the tourist industry. The combination of flight scheduling on the part of my airline, summer delays due to congested airspace and the knock-on effect it had on later flights in the day, as well as the work-to-rule action, meant that in one eight-day period only one late night-stopping flight managed to land in Inverness and as someone who relied heavily on these flights to get to work myself, I decided to wade in not only with my local MP but also with people I had got to know within my airline who were able to directly influence the ability to protect these flights. I did this for my benefit but also because I loved my job and working for my airline and I didn't want its reputation to be damaged by something controllable - this was resolved fairly quickly and means I am already someone who is known to Douglas and to my great surprise, he agrees to help us with our quest for charitable status.

I suspect his support was instrumental in the fact that we were granted charitable status in a record 21 days and so Project Wingman Foundation Ltd was officially born as both a business and a charity.

Another area in which we receive a lot of support is from the PR department at my airline. I have already been in contact with my airline Director of Flight Ops, David Morgan, to ask for his permission to allow the crew to wear their uniforms as part of this project, and not only has he agreed, but he has also offered to contact the DFOs at other airlines to smooth the way for their crew to do the same. This support alone is exactly what we need, but in addition, we have been assigned a member of the PR team to help with any interviews and press we may encounter. This is not entirely altruistic as it is in the interests of the airline to make sure that nothing is said that can reflect badly on them, and I have already been press trained by the airline as part of the making of the ITV documentary 'Inside the Cockpit' the previous year, so I already know Holly who will now be helping with press enquiries. This is mostly brilliant, but we also find it very restrictive as we are not allowed to talk to any press or media without permission and this is often not granted. Holly understands my frustration, but her hands are often tied, and she tries to help us as much as she can. I have also been building a working relationship with Phillip Allport who is director of external communications for Norwegian and he is extremely helpful and supportive in every way he can be. It is his support that leads us to an introduction to Anders Lindström who will go on to spearhead Wingman USA.

One of the things Dave and I have been adamant about has been making sure we have our own identity. Our volunteers are Wingman volunteers, and our lounges are Wingman lounges, we are very quick to make sure that any raids on this identity by individual airlines are squashed immediately. This is important because we believe there will be bad news from airlines in the future and we want to protect our volunteers and provide them with a 'safe space to fall' as part of the Wingman family whilst also keeping any potential airline politics away from the NHS we have committed to help. I believe we are successful in this whilst also being careful to keep the airlines on our side and as we gain traction, we start to gain their trust as well with me becoming the official spokesperson for the charity.

I do radio interviews with the BBC, and newspaper and magazine interviews with the Guardian and the Telegraph and word quickly spread about what we are doing. By the beginning of May, and just five weeks after founding Project Wingman we have around 2000 volunteers on our books and a rapidly growing back office team which includes a media department headed up by my friend and colleague Zoe, a Comms Team which links hospitals and Volunteers together and includes a friend from my command training, Lynsey, Esther, a BA captain called Geoff, and fellow Inside the Cockpit star, Stuart. We meet daily because the charity is moving at such a fast pace and there is always so much to do, organise and decide on. The time has also now come to move our attention away from London and we start to focus on other areas, spreading to Luton, Liverpool, Birmingham, the Scottish Borders, and my local hospital in Elgin on the Moray Firth.

Another member of our team is Mark, a Loganair pilot whom I have mostly got to know in the queue for security at Inverness Airport. We have become friends, and he has also now joined the team to offer support with the implementation of lounges.

One day I am on the phone with a Virgin Training Captain called Paul about some help he has offered in Edinburgh, and we are talking about his RAF career and mutual friends we have. During the conversation, we suddenly realise that we were on the same University Air Squadron in Yorkshire at the same time and so knew each other 25 years ago. Neither of us had realised until then especially because I am now a Henderson rather than my maiden name. That realisation is enough for us to swear undying support to each other forever especially where Wingman is concerned - and it is one of the many re-connections I will make as time goes on.

Word is now spreading fast and EmmaG, a friend and colleague from Stansted has also joined the team to handle donations. The simple premise we started with has changed rapidly as hospitals have been inundated with generous donations from members of the public - but they don't have the staff to be able to distribute these, so we step in to help, and our First-Class Lounges are born not only out of the generosity of the British Public but also corporate donations. We are given sound systems, banners, food and drink, plants, and balloon arches, and one company that comes on board offers to supply all of our lounges across the entire country with newspapers and magazines. Gold Key Media become friends and allies and also become our first founding sponsors to recognise their incredible generosity. By the end of our first year, Gold Key Media will have donated £7 million worth of newspapers, magazines and luxury items and will remain our single largest sponsor.

Now into May, we are all still in lockdown, all flights have been grounded for weeks and our crew volunteer base as well as the number of lounges has mushroomed. We have more than four thousand volunteers, our lounges have been spreading across the country and Dave and I, along with our teams have been working flat out with no respite for weeks. I have barely left my desk at the expense of my family who are starting to feel the strain. I don't go shopping, our adult daughters who are living at home as all their studies are now online do that, and the stress levels in our house with four people trying to use Wi-Fi that is dodgy at the best of times, are high. (We live in the countryside at the very end of a copper exchange and have been told that we will never get super-fast broadband. This has never been a problem before but now with everything being online, it is something that is all the more irritating because my parents, who moved to a house less than half a mile away are not only on a different exchange but have had fast internet for months. Jim eventually takes matters into his own hands and climbs onto our roof to install an aerial that will give us 4G Wi-Fi - it sort of works sometimes much to the disgust of our daughters who are not only stuck at home with THE most boring people in the world but are part of the generation who have no idea how to do anything if they can't do it online - it's going to be a long lockdown!)

One day the lid blows off the pressure cooker with some force and whilst I would love to say that we have an adult conversation about priorities and come to a civilised solution, no one who ever locked down with a military husband and two student girls would believe me. The fallout is immense - no one speaks for days other than to 'pass the salt' but the air has at least been cleared and I call Dave to tell him I am taking a weekend off and will not be contactable. His response is to tell me that, "Covid doesn't stop for the weekend and nor should we." I am livid but simply explain to him that I will be uncontactable for the weekend and will pick things up on Monday. There is a lot of work to do but if I don't take a break and spend some time with my family, two things will happen. I will burn out and be useless, and more importantly, I will find myself with no family to spend time with! That weekend is bliss. The weather is amazing and since we can't go anywhere, I spend a lot of time lying in the sunshine, doing stuff in the garden that is becoming my sanctuary, and sleeping. It is the reset I need, and I am ready to hit the ground running on Monday morning.

Before I go on, I should explain that I have a well-known hot tub in my garden - well known because in the ITV documentary in which I appeared in 2019, Jim pointed out that the hot tub was mentioned 5 times, the children once, and he wasn't mentioned at all... this is not deliberate on my part and I blame the editors! I am sure the bits where I mentioned him and told everyone what a great guy he is just ended up on the cutting room floor (that's my story and I'm sticking to it!). I bought the hot tub when we moved home to Scotland, after spending a month working in Porto. During that month, my family came out to stay with me and had their holidays there, although I was working, we were all together, and I was paid a lot for being there. Although I had days off, I didn't go on holiday that year and so I managed to persuade Jim to let me use the money to buy the hot tub and this means that now we are effectively locked down in a coastal garden spa. Never have we been more grateful for this bit of kit, and I spent a lot of this first weekend break, in there, just thinking. The hot tub is so well known that everyone at Wingman I think assumes I am in it all the time - it would be unprofessional of me to confirm how many meetings I end up holding in it but anyone who was ever in a meeting with me with the camera turned off will now know why!

As the month wears on, the first of our significant family events rolls around. We have four of them this year and we don't know if we will be able to celebrate any of them in the way we had planned. Jim is about to turn fifty and we celebrate, just the four of us, by having a cheese and wine-tasting evening, with dinner, in posh clothes. Our eldest daughter has decided that Friday nights are dress-up nights and we have dinners dressed as Pirates, a black-tie supper, and characters from the 70s and 80s (I go as Zippy and late that night decide that Zippy wants a turn in the hot tub - I can confirm that a full Zippy costume complete with head quickly becomes uncomfortably hot when wet!) and so it goes on. There is one other thing we do to celebrate this momentous occasion and that is go for a walk on the beach. We have not left the confines of our garden for 8 weeks and the trip to the beach complete with kites and a bottle of champagne is momentous.

Out of the blue, Dave announces his departure from the project, with immediate effect, to pursue an independent direction of travel. It is a blow, but we move on. The charity is gaining momentum and thanks to the support of my MP, Douglas Ross, we now have official charity status which has opened up more doors.

A conversation with the rest of the board leads to me being appointed CEO of the business and the charity and I build a team around me that I know will not only support me but also call me out if I am going in the wrong direction. I have almost no experience of anything to do with running something as big as this other than what I have learned as it has been built over the last few months and I take my lead from former easyJet CEO Dame Carolyn McCall who came into the airline from the Guardian newspaper. She knew how to run a business but had no airline experience, so she put people in place to advise her that knew everything she needed to know. The airline went from strength to strength under her tenure and I have always admired the way she did that whilst also making a point of getting to know as many employees as she could. I take my lead from her, and we form a new board with a great mix of experience to carry us into the future.

At first, I didn't want to be seen as the leader because I didn't want people to think I was bossing them around. Most of us on the exec team are pilots and many of us are captains - we all have enormous amounts of responsibility in our day jobs, and I try and create the flattest leadership structure that I can. There are so many facets to the charity now and we are rapidly trying to spread ourselves too thinly which is quickly sorted out by a fortuitous conversation with Tea Coliani who I know from the Women in the Hotel Travel and Leisure industry 'Women to Watch' awards. She puts me in touch with a company called Q5 which is doing pro bono work for charities set up during COVID and they agree to take us on and help us. Talking to them collectively and privately is like having a messy ball of wool that they neatly unwind, unravel and wind up into something sensible. We decide to take the path of doing 'less, well' (the comma there is important!) and our mantra is KISS - Keep it Simple Stupid - one that is very familiar to those of us in the aviation industry!

We focus on the lounges which now number more than sixty, recruiting and engaging with volunteers, and donations which are keeping the lounge stocked with goodies.

Around this time, I was put in contact with Anders Lindström who works for Norwegian in New York. He loves the idea of Wingman and wants to do something similar in the US. It doesn't take long to talk him through what is needed, and our only concern is that we don't know much about the American healthcare system other than that it is very different from our own NHS. Anders manages all of that and one afternoon I find myself in a meeting with the VPs of two NYC Medical Centres - Flushing and Jamaica, which are the first response centres for JFK and La Guardia - and they are very interested in what I have to say. As a result of that meeting, Wingman USA launched at these two medical centres and we hope that it will gain the same momentum it has in the UK but as US airlines never really stop operating, the crew numbers are not there, and the airlines seem unwilling to encourage their crews to go into hospitals to help.

By the end of July, things seem to be returning to some sort of normality, a lot of crew are returning to work and the government's formal furlough scheme which I have been on with most of my colleagues is changing significantly. This brings with it two issues, one of which is about to take an increasing amount of my attention. The first is that with volunteer numbers dwindling, we decide to make the decision to formally close many of the lounges which we do on 31st July and my friend Paul who has been running the Edinburgh lounge invites me down for the final day at Edinburgh Royal Infirmary, complete with the trust CEO, a representative from ScotMid, one of our biggest supporters in Scotland, and also Jonathan Hinkles who is MD of Loganair which has provided so many crew to us but also been generous and supportive in so many other ways. It is the first time I have left Morayshire and I drive down the A9, a road that is so familiar from 25 years of driving up and down, feeling like I am visiting a new planet! It is amazing how quickly our comfort zones shift from (in my case) the whole of Europe to a rural plot on the Moray coast.

The afternoon is fantastic, not only because I operate my

first Wingman shift in a uniform I have not worn for months, but also to see the immense gratitude from members of staff and management who are all so thankful for all we have done. It is good for me to be up close and personal with the things I have helped to create and seeing people who I am not related to for the first time in months is also a pleasure that I had not realised I had missed so much. At the end of the shift, the entire Wingman team is applauded as we walk out of the lounge and through the atrium and I am not ashamed to say that by the time I leave the building with Paul, at the back of the line of amazing aircrew volunteers who have given everything they have left to give over the last 3 months, I am in tears. These people have done this because they care, but they have also done it because in one way or another, I asked them to and that is something I haven't been able to comprehend not having been in a working lounge until now.

The second thing that I have to deal with is what I am going to do about my job. For eleven years I have worked for a company that I love, doing a job I not only adore but feel lucky to have, and as a family, we have both benefitted hugely from, but also made big sacrifices for me to be able to do. It is always the case that rockstar wages come with brain surgeon responsibility and the weight of this responsibility is heavy on my shoulders. The last few months have been busy for me with Wingman, but they have also been full of uncertainty about the future of my job. As soon as news of the pandemic started to hit the news I had an inexplicable feeling that it was going to be life-changing for all of us - and I struggled to believe airline management in the early days of them saying that the airline had plenty of money and there was nothing to worry about. I knew this to be true, but I also know that every day an airline doesn't fly costs it millions of pounds in lost revenue. I have also become very comfortable being at home all the time. This is something that people across the country will identify with and I have to think very carefully about whether I am just being lazy or whether the sense of dread I feel at the thought of going back to work is something more significant. There are two problems with me going back to work at this point and furlough has delayed me having to face either of them. The first is that I live on the Moray Firth, and I work at Gatwick. The reason for this is that it is the easiest place to get to on the whole network. People who have asked me in the past if it would be easier for me to be based in Edinburgh have never been further north than Edinburgh or driven up the A9 which is mostly a single-carriageway. This has never been a problem in the past because there have always been seven flights a day to one of the London airports with either easyJet or British Airways so getting to and from work has been easy especially since I have reduced my hours to 75% part-time. Gatwick was also my base of choice because two crews every night stay in Inverness giving me plenty of opportunities to effectively be working from Inverness rather than the other way round. Even though flights have started up again from some airports, there are still very few to and from Inverness and not enough for me to commute in the way I have previously.

There is so much uncertainty around what the future looks like, and I find it deeply unsettling. The pandemic has forced all airlines to make changes and the job I loved has already changed beyond recognition. I have too. It might be age or circumstance, but I no longer want my life to revolve around a roster that I have no control over. There are other factors too. Jim has an auto-immune condition that makes him vulnerable enough to have been told to shield. If I am to start travelling up and down the country again regularly, we will spend most of our time apart, and the time we are together I will not be able to see him or even sleep in the same room. It won't be forever, but it is no way to live after a quarter of a century of being married. Where's the fun in being married if you can't roll over in the middle of the night and prod your husband to stop him from snoring after all… the company puts out an email telling people that if they need to remain on furlough to protect a family member they should get in touch. I do this and am told that I need to provide evidence of Jim's condition. This is provided by the Senior Medical Officer on my husband's RAF base and the response from the company is staggering. According to the company doctor, and despite the government telling us that he needed to be protected, the condition is not serious enough for the company to support my request. I am furious, and if I am honest, one of the final threads that was keeping me tied to the company and the job I loved was cut with that phone call. The lack of empathy was astonishing, and I suspect I wasn't the only one in this position. There are other things too - I don't approve of senior management being awarded over a million pounds in shares as a bonus in a year when there had already been multiple redundancies, and I have always put my money where my mouth is - if you can't reconcile yourself to something you disagree with in an airline - or any industry actually - you have two choices, get over it, or get out. There is no room in a flight deck for a grumpy captain who strongly disagrees with the company they work for. By the time voluntary redundancies are announced Jim and I have been through every version of what the future might look like if I stay, and also if I decide to leave. Our wine bill has gone up considerably during these discussions - in fact, it has reached the point where the girls are complaining about having to buy so many bottles all the time so as responsible parents, we do the right thing and turn to the wonder that is Majestic with its weekly deliveries and exceptionally helpful phone operators who always have good ideas about what to try next...

When the company asks every pilot to consider taking a 50% contract, I know that if I take redundancy, I will also be saving the jobs of two of my colleagues, and by this time, three bases - one of which was Stansted where I had started - have been announced as being positioned for closure. This means that there is a fighting chance that my leaving, might just help to keep the jobs of two of my actual friends and the day the decision is made is more of a weight off my mind than I had realised it would be.

There is a process involved in leaving your job and I go through the motions of this in the same way that I would do anything I have been trained to do as a captain. It is just paperwork, but there are days when I am an emotional wreck. I know I am doing the right thing, but I never thought it would end like this. I suppose that I had imagined that I would stay working for my airline until I was either too old to legally work or too tired to continue, and I also imagined that I would have had time to say goodbye. Taking redundancy in the middle of a pandemic when travelling around is forbidden removes all of the fluff from this process and so it is that twelve years of operating as a co-pilot and then captain around Europe ended with the click of an electronic signature on an email document. I have no idea if I will ever set foot in a flight deck again - or if I will want to and as I finally pack up my ID card, company iPad, and Mobile phone (don't get too excited at this it is a very basic Nokia that has buttons which are so small they render anything other than actually making a phone call completely impossible which I think is the whole point of them!) and other paraphernalia into a protected box to post back to Gatwick, I feel a combination of a huge sense of relief as well as overwhelming sadness. I have worked hard to get to this point and although I never expected it to come to an end in this way, and the messages of support I receive from so many friends I have made throughout my career are so heartwarming, I have very little time to sit and navel gaze because I am busy with Wingman.

Throughout the summer we have been working on an idea that pops up in a meeting one morning and is instantly jumped on by all the men who are present! Someone suggests that we take Wingman on the road and this idea morphs into the possibility of using a converted double-decker bus to provide mobile well-being lounges. I am not in the least surprised when within nanoseconds of this suggestion even being made, I am being shown images of busses that are for sale - I have no idea how these have been found so quickly and have my suspicions that amongst our number are some closet bus fans who have just been permitted their fantasies to be unleashed. It is a frightening prospect but one that gains pace exponentially and I spend hours on the phone with one person especially who has taken this idea on board to the point where he thinks he can make it work. By the end of August, Rich has sourced what he thinks will be the perfect bus - it is already converted, has been used previously by a supermarket for cooking demonstrations, and is available for us to buy when we want it. Rich very quickly becomes Mr Bus and puts hours and hours into creating a business plan to present to the board to show what could be done. We all love it, and the idea passes board approval immediately - although there is one minuscule little snag. We have no money or almost no money. We have received very generous donations from members of the public, fundraising efforts amongst our number, and even a massive donation from a football club, and a lot of this has been used on provisions for the lounges and general running costs for the charity itself.

For the bus to work, having done everything we want to do to it, we need £100,000 and we need to raise this in the middle of a pandemic during which so many people, especially in our industry, have been either made redundant, taken reduced contracts (and therefore reduced pay) and well known, long-running charities have been suffering from lack of funds due to their shops and normal fundraising activities being shut down. We are a startup charity, hardly anyone knows about us, and no one has any fundraising experience. In what has become typical fashion for our charity, this doesn't worry us in the slightest and we put together a fundraising plan involving donated prizes and a crowdfunding campaign which we think will work.

Over the summer we get a couple of lucky breaks in terms of publicity when my MP Douglas Ross, who helped us to gain our charitable status, stands up in the Houses of Parliament and makes a formal request for the work of Project Wingman to be acknowledged and specifically mentions me by name. This is completely unexpected but generates more outside interest when people look us up. The request is met by a response from Jacob Rees-Mogg suggesting that we receive a copy of Hansard recording this public display of thanks and this is duly presented to our Team through Jess, Team Leader at Dr Grays Hospital in Elgin, by Douglas Ross himself. Failing to understand the importance of this event, I explain that I am unable to attend as I have a raft of meetings that morning and we have been told of this at quite short notice. I expect that was the wrong answer as I never get a response from Douglas again, but in his defence, he is quite a busy man!

A few weeks later, I receive a phone call from an office somewhere in Whitehall, telling me that I had been named as a 'Points of Light' recipient thanking me for my work during COVID, and receiving a certificate and a letter from the Prime Minister.

This is another opportunity for us to get some much-needed publicity and another complete surprise.

After this, more awards start to come our way for the work we have been doing and as the figurehead of the organisation (or Mother Hen as one of the directors calls me) I find myself on the guest list for numerous awards ceremonies made all the more surreal by the fact that they are all hosted online!

As for the bus, this morphs into a campaign that we name Wingman Wheels and as we enter another phase of relative normality, and lounges close as hospitals reclaim the spaces they had given over to our well-being lounges, our focus shifts to encompass the mobile element too.

In October we are approached by a large investment company and offered finance for the bus. It is a generous offer and one which we pursue initially - the idea being that the company would buy and own the bus and lease it to us for £1 a year. We enter talks with them about what this would look like in reality and eventually reach a sticking point. They are offering funding to the tune of £80,000 but there is a rub. They want the bus to be branded with their corporate identity and there is no room for negotiation on this. We agree unilaterally that we are not willing to rock up in a hospital car park with a well-being bus that has an investment company branding plastered all over it, and although it is a hard decision because we are making a lot of work for ourselves, we do the right thing and walk away. The charity has this at its heart, and this is something that I have always been keen to promote. It would have been an easy win to have this bus paid for by someone else, but there's no such thing as a free lunch and the price for their friendship is too high.

Our initial efforts to fundraise produce brilliant results. We have preplanned some of this so that when the crowdfunding opens on day one, we have a sudden dump of money into the account to the tune of £10,000. This has all the signs of being an amazing fundraiser that will meet our ambitious targets, but the challenge in the end just proves to be too great. Despite the best efforts of everyone involved, and they do go above and beyond for us, in the end, our total is just under one-third of what we needed, and I remind people that although it isn't what we are aiming for, it is still exceptionally good going for a tiny charity that has hardly any publicity. We do well with publicity when we are approached but we don't have contacts at the news agencies and other places that we need so all of the money we have raised has come from people we collectively know, and this makes the achievement all the more staggering. There is one contact we have from the very early days, who links us into some BBC Local radio slots, and this produces a little bit more momentum but without an actual publicist, we are doing the very best we can.

Early in December, just as the crowdfunder launches, I am sitting in a Zoom meeting which has become the norm for so many of us across the country. In the corner of my screen, a notification pops up from the Cabinet Office which I initially assume is spam. I am not exactly in the habit of receiving emails from government departments so why would they want to speak to me?

I click open the email expecting to file it in the bin when I realise that it is addressed to me. When people say their hearts have skipped a beat I always think it is a complete overreaction, but my heart feels like it has stopped for a second. I am looking at an email addressed to me, explaining that I have been nominated to receive an MBE from the Queen for my charitable works. I am usually fairly unshockable, but on this occasion, I am speechless which is probably a good thing because I am still in a meeting and the email specifically requests that I don't tell anyone at all about this upcoming honour.

I have to shut down the email and go back into the meeting but as soon as it ends, I go back and read the email again - it seems completely genuine and even I don't know anyone who could play a prank this realistically. My eyes leak a little as I re-read the email and then reply as requested to say that I would be delighted to accept such an honour - I had no idea that you have the right to turn it down, and even less idea why anyone would do that but people do! This is so exciting I don't even know how to respond, and it presents me with a big dilemma. I started talking when I was 10 months old, and have rarely stopped since, even talking in my sleep on occasions. In fact, during my initial command assessment flights, a lovely trainer who I got on very well with, told me that to learn how to become a captain, I was going to have to learn to talk less…I am not sure I ever did this, or at least not permanently, but at the time it was good advice. Now I am sitting looking at an email, containing the biggest surprise EVER, and being asked not to tell anyone for weeks! I consider having my jaw wired shut temporarily but realise that this would have other negative side effects, and in the run-up to Christmas, I would be depriving myself of the ability to eat my body weight in Ferrero Rocher which everyone knows is an absolute law from 1 December onwards, and decide that the only way I will be able not to tell anyone will be to deal with the admin side of it and then pretend it never happened.

Within three seconds of Jim getting home from work, I told him (I consider that the request to tell no one does not apply to my husband of 25 years from whom the only secrets I have are how much I spend on clothes every year, and also the fact that the cake I made him for his 24th birthday before we were married, although delicious, had actually slid off the plate and landed icing side down on the road as I was transporting it from my house to my car, and I spent hours picking bits of gravel out of the icing which I managed to patch up and no one knew a thing...until now) and sworn him to secrecy too. I trust that he will be much better at keeping this secret than I have been because that's his job. He sometimes has secret meetings which I always (hilariously I might add) ask him how anyone knows about, given that they are secret. He is so nice that he still laughs a tiny bit at me saying this - that's real loyalty.

There is one other person I eventually tell, and I am allowed to do this according to the email which states that if your media department needs to know about this upcoming award, you may divulge this information to them or similar wording. I say nothing at all for over a week and one day I call Zoe, my friend, fellow captain, and also our Head of Media. I tell her that I have something to tell her that she can't tell anyone else and am gobsmacked to find that she already knows! Or at least, she has guessed, because it turns out that she has been part of the team of people who have put together the nomination! The reason I need to tell her too is that it is going to generate a lot of media interest at exactly the time of year when she will quite rightly be busy with her family, and I reassure her that I will manage all of the media stuff so that she can continue to enjoy the festivities. Zoe doesn't work like that though and because she is fantastic and also super organised, she makes sure there is a press release available and ready to go at exactly 2200 on 30th December which is when the list is released. Zoe is amazing and has handled all of our media from the very beginning. She has learned on the hoof and picked it up very quickly and she knows exactly what, and more importantly, what not to say and this is no exception.

With three days to go, we are having a final and very precious family meal before our son leaves to return to work in London. We are lucky that he made it up for Christmas at all as he was airborne when the announcement was made effectively cancelling Christmas for thousands of families across the country, so we got to spend that precious time with him and before he leaves, I want to tell him, and the girls face to face about the award. They are all very proud and excited about it, and they wouldn't be my family if they didn't make sure my feet remain firmly planted on the ground by gently taking the piss out of me at the same time as showing their pride. The following day a photographer from the Press Association arrives at my house and we head to the beach for a photo shoot on a day that looks lovely but is freezing. I think my hands are going to fall off as we take photo after photo - and this sets a trend for the next few days as TV stations and journalists contact me to comment on the award. I am also invited to attend a cabinet office Press Conference which I do from the comfort of my landing, where my desk has been cunningly positioned in a run of worktop underneath a dormer window, and from where every piece of business that Wingman has conducted over the previous 9 months has taken place. This is a whole new world for me, and I would be lying if I said I hate it, I love every moment, knowing it won't last, and knowing that I have one chance to say what I need to for the benefit of the charity and more importantly the aircrew volunteers who are its beating heart.

I get my message across and go back to preparing dinner. We still haven't said anything to the rest of the family, and we decide that I will phone my brother-in-law at 2155, and Jim will phone his parents, and then we would post it on the family WhatsApp group, as well as texting my brother who lives in New Zealand. This is a fantastic plan, or at least, it would have been had our son not Face Timed and we were still talking to him when the Ten O'clock news came on and there was my face, not only on our TV screen but on the TV screens of millions of people across the country as headlines like, 'Airline Pilot Lands MBE' appeared on the BBC. The phone rang within seconds, and my brother-in-law cut to the chase saying, "Were you ever going to tell us?" I reply, "Sorry, who are you?" Just before I apologise to him for not managing to tell them in time.

The last time my phone was this red hot was in May 2019 when the first episode of Inside the Cockpit aired, and I watched from behind a cushion, not knowing what the edit would have done to the hours and hours of footage we had filmed. The messages of congratulations and shear love pour in, well into the night and for the next few days as the news spreads and I find myself not only overwhelmed once again by hearing how proud people are of me, but also immensely proud of myself of every single Winglet (as our volunteers have named themselves) and all they have achieved, because whilst this award is being given to me, it is really for every single member of the Wingman family who has given up their time, and put so much of themselves into helping the NHS and each other. There is no doubt in my mind that we have all pulled together and kept each other afloat during this storm, an analogy I have used often to try and encourage not just the Winglets but anyone who needs it, reminding them that we are not all in the same boat, but in very different boats in the same storm. This achievement is something we have all done collectively and so it belongs to all of us.

The media attention has given us the publicity we needed, and the crowdfunding gets some more interest over the next few days, but eventually, we have to bring it to an end and work out what we are going to do next.

The company that owns the bus is willing to give us an interest-free finance option, and at the suggestion of Carey Edwards who has been developing our Human Factors programme as well as championing the bus most valiantly, we approach NHS Trusts, knowing that we have provided them with so much for no fee for such a long time, and also knowing that there is money available to them from NHS Charities Together and the amazing Captain Tom campaign which is specifically set aside for staff well-being, and ask them to effectively make up the shortfall, by offering them the bus for two weeks at a time for a fee. The fee is not enormous in terms of what we could be charging but is also enough to give us the money we need to buy the bus outright, and this, along with a lot of goodwill from companies who are supportive, is how our mobile lounge project becomes a reality. All the work that Rich and his team have put in over the last 6 months comes to fruition on a cold February morning at the Homerton University Hospital NHS Trust in Hackney, North London, when the big blue bus that we have named 'Wellbee' rolls into position and becomes our first mobile lounge. The country has gone back into lockdown and so I am unable to be there to see it in action but the photos and videos that come my way bring it to life.

Two days later, a stroke of luck in a connection via one of our volunteers with a researcher on the BBC One Show brings us the TV gold we have been looking for when a film crew is sent to record a story for their show that evening, and this includes an interview online with me. Everyone is at their very shiniest and smartest for this event, and I break my normal tradition of not wearing make-up. I have rarely worn it for two main reasons, firstly I am very lazy with my appearance - I just can't be bothered to spend hours and hours putting on make-up, styling my hair, painting my nails etc, only to have to wipe it all off again hours later, and secondly,

I look like a clown when I wear it. I have never learned the art of 'Smokey eyes' achieving more 'beaten up panda', and anything that suggests it will make me look 'Sunkissed' is guaranteed to give me a slightly shiny orange glow. It is just easier all around if I don't bother, also, in fairness, I spend a lot of my time these days talking to plants so honestly, who would it even be for? I even wash and style my hair desperately trying to copy what the hairdresser does every couple of months to try and turn my tangled web of beachcomber's hair into something smooth and silky. I am happy with the result and enjoy talking about how Wingman was formed and what we do, and the way it is all presented that evening during the show is exactly what we have been hoping for with the classic ending of, 'It's not an Airbus, but a care bus,' becoming a slogan we will repeat over and over again.

Buoyed by this and the momentum we are once again gaining from people being at home, locked down and furloughed we start to make plans for our first birthday party - an online event organised by Esther, who makes us proud. Somehow, one of our directors, Mark, has managed to contact Liz Abram of Who Dares Wins, and persuade her to get involved as a compère and we film a scene where she 'catches' me relaxing in the hot tub and then interrogates me about the charity. It is shown on the night and is such a laugh to both film and watch, and sets the night up to be a brilliant success. Even more importantly we can give awards to some of our amazing volunteers for all their hard work - ideally, we would like to give everyone an award but that is simply not possible, and the evening is a resounding success as well as being very emotional.

The evening also marks one full year of Project Wingman and we have big plans for the future already underway, but as I sit there watching the awards being given out, and having the opportunity to tell everyone just how much it has meant to me as well as to so many others that we have all pulled together to support each other, and reminding them of just how far we have come in such a short period, I can look back and appreciate that something that started as an idea scribbled down in a notepad 12 months before, has become something really big, really special, and something that I really hope will last long into the future. We have become family. We have had highs - weddings, pregnancies, engagements, made new friendships that will last a lifetime and lows - we have lost people we love, some of us have lost jobs, there have been relationship breakups, illnesses and many other challenges, but we have got through it all together, different boats in a storm that is still raging, and having each other to lean on means everything.

Chapter Nine

Communication

Let's get one thing straight - delays piss us off as much as they do you and working for a budget airline, they happen ALL the time. This is mostly because of the amount of time allowed for a low-cost carrier to park on the stand, offload all the passengers, clean the cabin (carried out by cabin crew and sometimes assisted by the pilots), carry out all the pre-flight checks, load up the flight plan, unload and reload all the baggage, fill up with fuel and sometimes restock the bars for catering is 25 minutes. Yes, you read that right - 25 minutes. The fact that this is achieved 95% of the time is remarkable and a testament to the ability of the crews and ground crews to get everything done. Next time you pull on to stand, leave the aircraft, step onto a bus, walk through to baggage reclaim and leave the airport, have a look around at all the people who are making that happen - it is a work of art when it goes right, and a complete shitshow when it goes wrong.

The most important way that pilots can help to either make this run smoothly or placate people when they don't is really simple. Communication. It is one of our 'soft skills' that we are graded on in our six-monthly simulator checks, and our bi-annual line checks, and it is what we are judged on by our passengers and crew members at the end of the day too. We could be the best pilots in the world, slipping the aircraft onto the runway like a cat pissing on velvet (in the most eloquent words of my friend

Kev) every single flight, but if the captain doesn't communicate with the crew or the passengers, it will not even be noticed because the thing that will stand out will be the fact the captain is a grumpy git. This is not entirely fair because not everyone feels comfortable standing in front of two hundred people and talking to them through a slightly dodgy PA telephone designed in the 1980s, and since 9/11 all of this has been made much harder by the closing and locking of the flight deck door during flight and when the engines are running. The halcyon days of cabin crew pulling back the curtain and popping their heads around to ask if anyone wants a cuppa are long gone along with all the legendary stories (mostly from long-haul pilots) that went with them and we are now resigned to the fact that once the first engine is running, the flight deck door MUST be closed and secured until the last engine is shut down on the stand. There will be times when passengers can still visit the flight deck - and this is always during a delay - it is a nice thing for pilots to be able to do, showing you around our daily office, and to passengers, it is often a once-in-a-lifetime opportunity. We are allowed to do this as long as our engines are not running so the chances are that if you step inside a flight deck on your travels, you will be experiencing a reasonable delay. It passes the time and frankly, pilots are big show-offs (I make no exceptions here including myself). We love to show you the hundreds of switches, circuit breakers, screens, panels and thrust levers, and if we are lucky enough to be Airbus pilots, tray tables. This is the biggest gift any aircraft designer ever gave to pilots after installing autopilot. I don't care what any Boeing pilot tells you about being able to 'get the feel of the aircraft' through the yoke they have in front of them - they are all jealous because when I eat my lunch or dinner (and sometimes, breakfast, lunch and dinner all on the same flight!) I get to eat it at a table that pulls out in front of me, instead of having to balance it on my lap. This is so civilised that there was a captain I flew with at Stansted called Giles. He was French and behaved like all French men behave in my imagination - he was charming, courteous, a little bit naughty, and had so much respect for his mealtimes that he ALWAYS pulled out a clean and freshly pressed white napkin, a tiny cruet set, and a silk carnation that he slotted into his pen holder to make his eating area look just as it should! He was a laugh to fly with and I always loved his insistence that just because we were at 37,000 feet, his standards shouldn't have to slip!

We love to show you our world because we are proud of it and because it is something you don't often get to see, but it also serves another purpose. I have spent hours waiting for air traffic control restrictions to allow us to depart into the most congested skies in the world, hours sitting on the ground when my passengers could have lost their sense of humour, and made it a really difficult day for my crew, but this has never happened on one of my flights because I have always invited passengers into the flight deck to have a look around, sit in my seat (I usually let the very keen first officers do that actual talking just as I did when I was in that seat!), and gone into the cabin to talk to my passengers and help my crew - usually by handing out glasses of the finest water the aircraft water system has to offer. It's not much but it means a lot to people who are trying to explain to their tiny children why they are not going on holiday just yet, and even to very important business people who may not make their meetings, somehow a visit to the hallowed tiny room at the front of the aircraft (I don't mean the bulkhead!) seems to change the mood in a way very few other things can.

The other thing I have always prided myself on has been to keep passengers and crew updated with what is happening - even if there is not much to say - the fact that someone is talking to them, reminds them that we are working hard at the front of the aircraft during a delay to do everything we can to get them into the air - because that is where we want to be as well as you!

Everyone involved in getting an aircraft into the air and back down safely are part of one big complex team usually spread across numerous countries, but teamwork only happens at its best if communication is good in the first place. Of course, on an aircraft there are many ways of communicating, and one of them is over the radio.

There are two switches you can use in an Airbus to operate the radio and one handheld microphone. One is on the control column we use to fly the aircraft, and the other is a toggle switch on the main console, and most of our transmissions are done using these switches. We have two frequencies that we monitor while we are flying - the active frequency of the air traffic control unit that is controlling us at the time (although a lot of this is now done digitally rather than by voice which took some getting used to at first but was life-changing when flying through busy London airspace with weather around because using voice it is often hard to get a word in - even for me!) and the emergency frequency. This frequency is something we must all listen out for all the time, and sometimes it is used by aircraft that have lost contact with the correct frequency to get them back to who they are supposed to be talking to, sometimes it is used for training purposes by private pilot students who are practising what they would say if they were lost, and some of the time it is silent, apart that is, from the meowing - yes, that's right, the noise a cat makes. Many, many long night flights home have been broken up with the noise of cats meowing at each other much to the amusement of some and the great irritation of others. There is a certain nationality of pilots who are suspected of being the main culprits of this meowing, but it would be wrong of me to name them - (you know who you are!) but what is funny about this is the amount of times when the meowing will go on for some time, and then some very irritated (always male) captain from some unknown aircraft will come onto the frequency and say, "STOP this childish behaviour, this is the emergency frequency and you are blocking it with your irresponsible and stupid noises - you are a disgrace to your profession and you should be ashamed of yourself etc..." This is of course a fair point, it is the emergency frequency after all, but in broadcasting this rant to everyone in that large piece of airspace, the grumpy reply has done two things - firstly it has blocked the very frequency it is claiming to be protecting for much longer than it takes for someone to say 'meow', and secondly it always launches a cacophony of more 'meows' and despite the point being correct, it is really hard to keep a straight face - I don't know who those pilots are but I suspect that meowing on the emergency frequency is a tradition that will continue in perpetuity - I like to think so anyway.

The other way we communicate in the flight deck is using another 1980s handset we have installed which allows us to speak to the cabin over the PA system. We would usually use this once a flight to tell our passengers what time we expect to arrive, what the weather is like when we get there, especially if it is nice, and where we are now if there is something of interest which there usually is - Europe is smaller than you think, and there are a lot of cities you can point out from seven miles up in the air. On a clear night, flying back into London, from the south-east, there is one place in particular that is like a homing beacon for those of us who are coming to the end of a long day out to Tel Aviv, or Cyprus, or the Greek Islands and that is Belgium. Belgium stands out because whilst all the countries around it are interspersed with small blocks of light showing where the towns are, many of which go dark after around 10 pm, Belgium is lit up like a Christmas Tree - it seems that every street in every part of that country has a street light on it which is permanently on - and it is a welcome sight because by the time we get to Belgium we will probably have started initial descent into London airspace which means we are nearly home.

Anyway, back to the communication - this 1980s PA phone is stored in a completely different location to the handheld microphone that can be used for the radio, but you would be surprised at how many times people make a lovely speech ostensibly to their passengers, only to find that they have broadcast it to everyone on the radio frequency they are on instead. On quiet days this is met with a round of 'nice speech', 'well done', 'thanks for the info', and a lot of sniggering, on busier days it is a nightmare because it blocks the frequency for everyone else and this is not good. Usually, this is something that only happens once, you tend to remember it well enough not to do it again, and on the occasion when it happened to me, I was flying with my friend Toby. We always had a good day out and were often told that the passengers several rows back could hear us laughing (and thankfully appreciated the fact that we got on so well). Toby is a good-natured, extremely talented pilot, (and as it turns out, artist). We had just crossed the Brest Peninsular when I declared that I was going to speak to the passengers - Toby took control of the aircraft as is standard when the pilot flying is doing something else, and I could hear the cogs in his brain moving as he tried to decide which trick he would play on me today - would it be the hilarious pushing of the lever on my seat meaning it lowered to the floor? Or would it be writing something rude on the scratch pad to try and make me laugh during my PA - I was wise to Toby by this time and of course, far too much of a steely-eyed professional to be distracted by these kinds of antics and I was ready for him. My PA was astonishingly good (it probably wasn't at all but that's how I choose to remember it and since none of you were there you can't disagree...) so I was completely surprised when Toby suddenly reached over to my side of the centre console and hit the radio button. I stopped my PA and said, "What did you do that for you loony!" He just rolled his eyes and told me that I had delivered my PA to everyone on Brest Control and that although they all appreciated it, maybe I should try using the PA instead - I looked into my hands at the handheld radio microphone and hung my head in shame. It had happened to me too! It took several minutes for us to stop laughing about my stupid mistake before I could try again, and I had to do the entire PA deliberately looking out of the window in the opposite direction to Toby because he had, and still has, that ability to make me laugh out loud for no reason at all! The passengers of course had no idea that this was the second time I had read out all the information I had to give them, and I am not even sure if any of them listened to it anyway, but I am sure that all the pilots who were flying through Brest airspace on that day as well as the controllers were interested in the route we were taking to Faro!

Of course, it is a simple fact that more importantly than being defined by the jobs we do, we are all human and all of us get things wrong sometimes. There are many, many procedures in place to make sure that the things we get wrong are small and largely inconsequential, but they are a good indicator of how we are feeling generally. Making a PA on the radio frequency is something that happens to everyone, but if I had then gone on to make other small errors that could well have been a sign that I was becoming fatigued, or that something else was going on that needed addressing. The responsibility we carry as pilots, especially as a captain, is enormous, and the weight of it rests heavily on our shoulders even in the lighter and funnier moments of our jobs - and we all have to learn to laugh at ourselves at times. The communication skills we build on day after day in our jobs have also been extremely useful since leaving my airline and have been instrumental in the way that we have managed to build up a team, set up a charity and run it for 4 years with no prior experience. I am as comfortable talking to VPs of US medical centres as I am talking to the parking attendant in my local hospital and this all boils down to one thing which is respect. I have always had respect for everyone I speak to, whether it is a crewing officer calling me at 0330 to tell me I am needed for a duty, a member of my crew who needs me to help them with something, one of our amazing volunteers at Wingman who has something to say and deserves to be heard, or indeed a TV or Radio interviewer recording a piece about our charity, or a Sir or a Baroness, everyone is the same unless they prove themselves to different - what I mean by that is that everyone is equally deserving of my respect, and deserves to be treated in a way that I would like to be treated and for me, this is the secret of good communication. It doesn't matter who you are talking to as long as you are polite and respectful, anything you say, will be sincere. This is what has allowed me to build teams with everyone I have had the privilege of working with over the years, and what ultimately has allowed me to build and grow my charity into what it has become today.

Communication is everything, and if you can laugh at the times you get it wrong and then go back and do it again properly, learn from it and move on, you can create an open and honest dialogue with anyone around you, and the sky will be your limit.

Chapter Ten

Cabin Pressure

While we are getting things straight, let me dispel a few myths about female pilots! Firstly, there is a reason why you don't often see a woman at the controls of a passenger, or any other, aircraft and that is simply that there are not very many of us. Even though over one hundred years ago, trails were being blazed by the likes of Amy Johnson, Amelia Earhart, Jean Batten and Beryl Markham, and the female ferry pilots of the Second World War, today, it remains a fact that less than 6% of the world's pilots are women, and only 3% of the worlds commercial airline pilots are women. There are far fewer female airline captains in the world than there are endangered Bengal Tigers (fewer than five hundred captains to two thousand tigers). The reasons for this are not completely clear, and not what I want to talk about in this chapter, but during my flying career, and since I have stopped flying, I have spent as much time as I can as a STEM ambassador, going into schools and talking to Brownie and Scout groups about keeping an open mind when it comes to attaching gender to an occupation because if we don't educate, nothing will ever change.

When I decide I want to fly, it has nothing to do with being a female pilot, and I don't come up against any barriers from anyone I know about doing that. I want to be a pilot. Period. It doesn't matter to me or anyone else that I am a woman, I am just as capable of pulling a Cessna or a Warrior out of a hangar and refuelling it as anyone else, and it turned out that I was equally as capable of learning my way around the inner workings of an Airbus - or as much as anyone can understand an airbus - there is an in-joke about Airbus (which I suspect came from Boeing pilots) that you never really know what an airbus is doing - this is simply not true and having never flown the Boeing, I never really understood this aversion to fly-by-wire aircraft - so the control column is an electric switch and the thrust levers don't physically move with every adjustment made by the engine management system known as FADEC as they do on a Boeing - none of that matters - it's all displayed right in front of you and makes perfect sense to me! It has always struck me that it is more important to have the right person doing the job than what their gender, race or religion might be - for me this is normal, but not for everyone. It is also important I think, when championing the cause of getting more women into the industry, not to disenfranchise the men! It is no more their fault that they outnumber their female colleagues by 33 to 1 than it is that a fish can't climb a tree, and more to the point, men LOVE having more women in the industry and actively encourage and support their female colleagues. In supporting the argument that there should be equality there needs to be a change at the top to do away with the misconception amongst certain training managers that airlines can only be run by ex-military fast jet pilots or anyone who can grow a beard without being considered scary to small children at least... and most of my male colleagues would thoroughly support that. The trouble is that often, equality comes as a result of huge inequality in the other direction and that has to be avoided at all costs. I don't approve of women being given jobs to get the numbers up any more than I approve of men being given jobs through nepotism - it has to always be on merit. There is another problem with this though which is that as a woman working in a world traditionally inhabited by men, we put a lot of pressure on ourselves to exceed anyone's expectations. A sim check that results in a row of 'Achieved Company Standard' remarks would have left me feeling disappointed with myself for not doing better - the airline might not need me to achieve more than this, but I do - I want to be 'Above Standard' or even 'Very Good'. On receiving a simulator report one year, I saw the words 'Very Good' next to some of the areas on which we were assessed and was peeved because I had always scored 'Above Standard' in these areas before. I was coming up to Command and wanted to do my very best and assumed that Very Good wasn't quite good enough to be Above Standard. On looking up the grades in the training manual I was shocked to find that Very Good was not only a higher grade than Above Standard, but that I hadn't known about it before! They are only words at the end of the day and always completely subjective but I hung a lot on those reports, and put a lot of pressure on myself to get everything right in the training devices which are our simulators - machines that closely resemble AT-ATs and being full motion simulators, can replicate as closely as possible the sensations of being in an actual moving aircraft. Although there was a requirement to pass, this is a pressure that I put on myself and although I have always felt that the training department was exceptionally good at ensuring that the training we received was not only meaningful but delivered in a very nurturing way, I never fully relaxed in the simulator - it was always an ordeal for me and there was only one occasion when I left simulator training feeling as if I had nailed it and had fun - and that was on command course two as I named it - the one I passed, the one in which my body and my pride didn't let me down.

Throughout my career I have been largely fortunate also, not to have come across the frankly quite shocking and pathetic attempts at intimidation or predation that still alarmingly exist throughout the profession I love - there is an incident, later described as a 'misunderstanding' in my early flying days, brought about as much by my naivety as the abuse of a position of leadership, although my naivety doesn't excuse the behaviour of the other party - needless to say, I learn that day that it is never a good idea to debrief a sortie in ones room in the Officers Mess, however hot the day, and however desperate for a cold beer. The very purposeful introduction a few days later to the wife of my instructor at the time is not so much threatening as a clear shot across the bows - don't speak of this again, and don't ruin my marriage. This might have been more easily achieved by a simple apology and a promise never to behave in this way again, but I will never know. Either way, whilst it irritates me, it doesn't deter me, and I never again agree to debrief anywhere other than a proper briefing room, always choosing to draw a firm line between my professional life and my personal one. Although for me, this is an isolated incident, I have been shocked and saddened over the years to hear stories from the many, many female colleagues I have got to know that paint a slightly different picture - but for me, other than this occasion, I was treated in the same way as my male colleagues. The airline industry does some of this well - I am and never have been seen as a female pilot by the rostering team or crewing - or at least not on paper. I am a number on a spreadsheet, a tiny cog in a very big wheel, simply a pilot who can either be used to fly or not. I am paid the same as my male colleagues and just as likely to get called off a 3 am standby. The ONLY time that I am considered differently comes down to my personality rather than my gender, and that is because I make an effort to get to know the people who work in these departments when I am working at Luton. On a normal day, our paths don't cross, but on a challenging day I could end up speaking to people from Operations, Flight Planning, Crewing, Engineering, and even the Duty Pilot, and these people can contact me via a texting system in the flight deck called ACARS - we can send messages back and forth if we need to - and I always made a point of going up to their office at the end of one of these challenging days with a box of chocolates or some biscuits to say thank you to them for working their socks off to get us home safely or with a smaller delay, or for sorting out whatever it is they have been working on for us. This was an Emma thing though, not a girl thing and I know some male colleagues did the same. It's basic manners!

I spend eight years on the ground in between the early days

of flying training on a squadron and resuming flying training at a flying club at Whenuapai in Auckland, New Zealand, where we have been posted for a 3 1/2-year exchange tour. Whilst my husband operates the P3 Orion for the mighty 5 Squadron RNZAF, I drop my tiny babies at school, pre-school and crèche and take flying lessons. I attract more attention for being a determined mother of three small children, and the time and dedication we give to the flying club as social secretary and CEO (my husband joins in the fun as well) than I do for being a woman. It is not particularly refreshing or enlightening because it is normal. There are lots of women in the RNZAF including a brilliantly fun lady I became friends with called Kelly - New Zealand's first female fast jet pilot - she is a legend, and utterly humble about everything she has achieved. I find New Zealand to be light years ahead in terms of its attitude towards women in the circles in which I mix. I understand this is not the case across all of New Zealand society but no one bats an eyelid when I tell them I am going to get my license while I am here - to be fair, the people I know are such an amazing bunch of achievers that no one bats an eyelid when, being overweight, a heavy smoker and have never run before, I give up smoking and declare I am going to start competing in triathlons, and run the Auckland half marathon - in six months - in fact, rather than question this, most of my friends decide to turn up at 5 am on the beach at Mission Bay to cheer me on as I plunge into the water for my first swim.

I am seen simply as a pilot in New Zealand, and I meet quite a few other female pilots of all ages while I am there, even when

I return to the UK, the number of female instructors at High Wycombe where we move to seems to be roughly the same as the number of males. We are all pilots and in that environment, as flight instructors, we all judge each other (for want of a better word) for all the stupid mistakes and hilarious stories we glean from our students!

It is only when I join the hallowed world of the airlines that I start to notice that as a woman, I stand out. For a start, I have the unfair disadvantage of everyone knowing my name! There are no other female flying instructors at the two flying schools I work at on the Moray Coast in Scotland, and so once people have met me, they automatically know my name and use it all the time breaking the code of not using someone's name on the radio all the time! I have often replied to a, 'Hey Emma,' over the radio with a, 'Hey, great to hear you, hope you are well,' whilst thinking, 'I wish I knew who you are!'

My first real brush with any sort of challenge came when I was doing some very early training in the simulator. Before you even get your hands on an aircraft type rating, you have to do something called MCC and JOC - these stand for Multi-Crew Co-operation and Jet Orientation Course. I am paired up with a sim partner who goes on to become a good friend, and we are sitting in a brief before a sim detail. As part of this, the instructor asks a little about us, and seeing my address asks why I live in Morayshire. A lot of the older instructors on this course are ex-military and almost everyone knows about RAF Kinloss and the Nimrod which is still operational at the time although little do we know that its glory days are about to come to a sudden end. I explain that I am a military wife and when asked about children, that I have a 7-, 9- and 11-year-old. I don't see the relevance of this to the sim briefing but am making polite conversation. Also, I miss my children a lot having never really left them before, so being on this course in the first place is something I am constantly questioning. The response from the instructor is unexpected at best and unwelcome at worst. "You should be at home with your children, not wasting your time here." Words that many years on are still burned into my mind. This is not the way to start a training session in the sim and my sim partner is as angry as I am that this has happened. I brush it off and get on with the job and although I flag it up with another instructor, this is the last time I am ever spoken to by any of my colleagues in a way that is anything other than with the mutual respect we have for each other. I later find out that this instructor's wife had recently died and he has a lot of regrets about spending time away from home - there is almost always a reason for the way that someone speaks to you, and from this, I learn that it is important sometimes, to choose not to be offended by something and have a little compassion for someone who may have simply been trying to say, "Don't miss out on your children," however it may have come across.

Whilst I only ever experience respect after this from my colleagues, passengers are a different story altogether, and again, it is important to understand that seeing a female pilot in the first place is a rare thing unless you happen to fly a lot. Many passengers fly once a year at most, and so are unlikely ever to come across a female pilot let alone a captain.

Most of the time, the comments passengers make are nice ones - complimenting me on a smooth flight (like I control the air) or for being early (without realising this just means they will be waiting longer for their bags!) - but sometimes, the comments have potential to offend. "Great flight love, but who parked it," "I hope you don't have to reverse," or "Well done for landing love," which I did once facetiously reply to with, "I have been doing it for thirty years, I ought to know what I'm doing by now." Most of the time I smile graciously and laugh back, aware of the fact that because it is so unusual to see a female captain, people want to say something to acknowledge this fact, but often don't know quite what to say - so making a comment about parking or driving in their minds, is better than saying nothing at all. I always choose not to be offended by this because I genuinely never believe that it is meant as anything other than an acknowledgement of the fact that I am not a man and therefore not who they are expecting to see. It helps that I am tall and what I like to describe as being 'well built', but also that I just don't worry about these comments or see them as being derogatory.

I do get to have some fun with this too of course. There are few days when we have a completely female crew on board, but on those rare and hallowed occasions, I like to welcome my passengers onto 'this unmanned flight' - that always gets their attention, and I can't claim credit for the saying - that belongs firmly with my friend and colleague Marnie!

On another occasion, I am sitting in the flight deck running through the brief with my first officer. We are going to somewhere like Malaga or maybe one of the Balearic Islands, and as it is a warm summer day, I have the flight deck window open to let in some air. Through the window, I hear a commotion coming from the aircraft step and look out to see a bit of a scuffle. Always fiercely protective of my cabin crew, I put on my jacket (for added authority and effect you understand!) and step into the cabin to ask if everything is ok. Some of the passengers boarding the aircraft are complaining about the behaviour of one man in particular and I decide to have a word with him before he steps on board. Just as I reach the door, another passenger comes on board visibly upset because his hat and glasses have been knocked off by the passenger I am concerned about. I apologise profusely, offer him a glass of water and reassure him that I will deal with it. The passenger who has caused the fuss is tall, cocky, very full of himself, and looking rather pleased with his behaviour, until that is I ask him to step to the side as I would like a word with him. I have a massive advantage and secret weapon in this case because by now, I have three teenagers, two of which are girls and I am very well practised in dealing with crap behaviour (actually that's unfair - my children have and never would behave in this way in public let alone on an aircraft, but what parent hasn't had to grit their teeth and try and work out how to bollock their child without making the situation worse?!). I ask the passenger to explain what has just happened (having seen it all from the flight deck window) and when he lies to me and tells me someone else started it, I explain to him that if I am not satisfied that he doesn't present a threat to the safety of my aircraft and flight, he won't be coming with us. He sneers at me and laughs as he looks down and says, "Oh yeah, we'll see what the captain has to say about that won't we..." I will never forget the look on his face when I reply, "I am the captain and you have two choices - you can either apologise to me and the passengers you have upset and come on board, or you can go back down the steps and I will offload you." As the captain, I have this right - I don't use it often but I am more than happy to - there is never a place for rudeness, especially not on board an aircraft and I earned the respect of my crew on many occasions because I always had their backs when it came to making difficult decisions like this. As it happens on this occasion, the passenger looked suitably embarrassed, apologised immediately to me, almost simpering as he made his way to apologise to the person he had been rude to and behaved like a suitably chided schoolboy to wherever it was we were going.

I never enjoyed telling people off on board (always passengers and only once a crew member), but I was always very aware that I wasn't there to be anyone's friend. My role on board the aircraft was to be its Commander and everything that went along with that. If that meant offloading someone, then I would do it and if it meant confronting bad behaviour, like the businessman who continued to carry out a very loud phone call during my welcome on board announcement, and the many occasions when people were drunk onboard and harassing other passengers - don't do that by the way, it is a criminal offence for which you can not only be nicked but banned from flying by not only the airline on which the offence is committed but every other airline operated by that state - they quite rightly all collaborate when it comes to disruptive passengers because there is no place for them at 37,000 feet.

I never set out to be anything other than the best pilot I could be, but it is inevitable when there are so few of you, that you end up taking on a kind of responsibility to fly the flag for the next generation of women who aim to sit where you sit, and I have many proud memories of times when people specifically said that they had felt safer knowing there was a woman at the front - it is psychological of course because we are all trained to the same very high standards and we are all tested and checked with the same regularity, but for some people, especially those who felt in some way nervous (and around 10% of passengers fall into that category) there was a perception that a woman would be somehow less likely to take risks than a man, and for me, if that made them feel safer and more comfortable on board, it didn't matter what the reason was.

It is also inevitable that as a human being, you will sometimes get things wrong, and this is when the only course of action, once you have corrected the mistake, is to laugh at yourself. One of the things that is most often commented on to me about Inside the Cockpit is the day that I got lost in Amsterdam. The lovely Stephen Fry smugly commentates that due to my error, we are left facing in the wrong direction (I had a female first officer and this clip was immediately followed by the hero boys landing in

Innsbruck which requires special training) which was frankly complete bollocks but made a much better story for the TV than, 'they went to the next junction down which worked just as well for the Air Traffic Controller.' I could have got the hump about that - but I chose to laugh at myself - I mean whatever - I had to wait for my stand to become available anyway so it didn't matter to us or the Tower and Stephen, I forgive you because the rest of your narration was quite good!

I didn't set out to be any of these things that I have become, but I am still a champion of anyone who wants a bit of support on their journey to the skies, a beacon of inspiration to some - perhaps, but ultimately, I will always be simply a pilot, and one who is proud of the job I did, and the way I looked after people along the way. And to my children, I will always be that big show off whom they laugh at and keep grounded, which is probably exactly what I have always needed from them!

Chapter Eleven

Tales from the Flight Deck

It is a well-known thing amongst aviators and their friends and families, that you will always know when there is a pilot in the room because they will tell you - this is a pretty fair assessment and I have met very few people who have been genuinely humble about what they do with one exception. From 2003 - 2006 we lived in New Zealand as my husband was a military exchange officer to the Royal New Zealand Air Force, and it was while we were living there that I picked up my ambition to learn to fly once more. My father-in-law was the Treasurer of the 617 Dambusters association, and on one visit since I had gained my private pilot's licence not long before, he asked me to fly him to Tauranga on the east coast of the North Island to meet a man called Les Munro. We flew down for lunch and Les and I not only became friends, we remained in contact until he died in 2015 - he was a champion of female pilots, and his granddaughter (also called Emma) was learning to fly at the time too. Les hadn't flown for many years, but there were two remarkable things about him. The first was that he was the last remaining original Dambusters pilot, and the second, more incredible thing was that after the Second World War was over, he returned to New Zealand, and his family didn't know what he had done until sometime in the 1960s even though he had been awarded a DFC for his wartime flying. He didn't talk about it much and he was a truly humble man - on the odd occasion when he did talk about it, his stories were the stuff of legend that I and many of my colleagues grew up imagining we could do!

Pilots (me included) are, on the whole, people who like to talk about their jobs and there is a very good reason for this. There are not many of us, and our jobs are cool. Seriously, just think about it for a second - when you are sitting sipping your G&T down the back, and wondering whether to have the Lobster Thermidor (or cheese sandwich if you are low cost as I was!) we are in control of a 70+ tonne aircraft and we know the purpose of every switch, and every circuit breaker and everything on board. It is a position of great responsibility, and we carry that responsibility with a great deal of care. We are also human however, yes, even those self-defined sky Gods who fly the mighty A380 are human. We all have homes to go to (contrary to what some people think we don't live at the airport although it feels like it at times, and we don't sleep on our aircraft either!) - we are all human, and sometimes, because of that, we get things wrong. These things are usually on the ground, and when in the air, because of the highly regulated nature of our jobs, almost always limited to mistakes we make on the radio, like talking to the passengers on the radio frequency and in one case, telling a plane load of passengers headed for Ibiza what the weather was like in Palma - I think this may have been the only time my passengers listened to the cruise PA! The results are rarely serious and often the only people that know are the flight crew themselves. I am talking about really low-level stuff here - like the time that, having landed at Luton, on a dark and wet night, we taxied straight past the stand we were supposed to be parking on as it was so difficult to see, and had to do a loop of the terminal - we decided that there was no way we could get away with this so the captain (I was a first officer at the time) made a hilarious and self-deprecating announcement which won everyone over and hopefully prevented a whole raft of complaints - honesty on these occasions is always the best policy).

Although the job itself is serious and MUST be taken seriously, there are times when there are lighter moments, and it would be fair to say we take the opportunity to see the funny side of things whenever possible. On one occasion, I was flying with a Captain who had been shipped up from Gatwick for a day, and because we had the same surname he spent the entire day introducing me as his co-pilot and wife!!! The passengers loved it, and we played to the crowd - the day passed in a flash, and we laughed even more when one chap commented as he was leaving the aircraft that he thought the captain must be a brave man to be locked in such a small room with his wife all day!

On another occasion, on realising that my colleague sounded exactly like Tony Blackburn of Radio DJ fame, we decided to spend the entire day making all our radio calls in the style of an enthusiastic 1980s DJ - it made us laugh, a lot, and far from being unprofessional as some will declare, it was a bit of harmless fun that we could switch on and off at will to pass the time of day - you see, although our jobs are super cool and we love them, there are parts of the day that go quite slowly and between take-off and landing, there are long stints of doing very little. We fly on autopilot along a pre-loaded route - and we monitor everything - we monitor the weather at our destination, we monitor the traffic around us using onboard traffic alerting technology, and we monitor the radios, always listening out on our given frequency for instruction from Air Traffic Control, as well as always monitoring the emergency frequency. We have time to eat food, drink cups of tea, and read newspapers - but never books - you get too absorbed in a book, you can dip in and out of a newspaper, and often, we don't read anything at all, we sit and chat about anything and everything - it can be a very sociable job when you have the right crew, and a very lonely one when you don't.

A well-known saying amongst aviators is that there are old pilots and there are bold pilots, but there are no old, bold pilots! On the whole, pilots are not risk-takers. We have systems on board our aircraft for example that show us what the weather is like on our routing, and if it looks as if it might be bad, we just fly around it - we don't enjoy sitting in turbulence any more than you do, we just understand it better, and we also understand what our aircraft are capable of. I have flown through some pretty bad turbulence over the years, but I have never been afraid, although I have always kept the passengers and crew safe by asking them to fasten their seatbelts until we are back in smooth air again. There has only been one occasion when I have questioned whether or not we should be in the air - and by the time I was questioning it, it was too late. I had been a captain for about a year and had been sent to Stansted for a check flight to make sure I was doing all the things that were expected of me in the left-hand seat. I was flying with a friend - most of the people I flew with at Stansted I am lucky enough to call friends because I spent my first 5 years there and because it was a small base, we flew together often. On this particular day, a storm was brewing - it had been named Doris and we were operating to Amsterdam and back and then up to Glasgow and back. I was already expecting not to be able to operate to Glasgow because the crosswind was forecast to go out of limits, but Amsterdam was looking ok - and you fly until you can't, but you always try. Earlier in the day, a KLM aircraft had made a heavy landing due to the wind in Amsterdam and its nose gear had collapsed on the runway, but when we landed, the wind was strong but steady, and down the runway. For the return flight to Stansted, the wind was once again, strong but coming from a reasonably sensible direction and we had LOADS of fuel on board. This is important because when the weather might prove to be a problem you need to have options. In this case, we had enough fuel to fly back to Amsterdam or divert to almost anywhere in the UK and we set off happy that the wind, although strong, was going to be within our limits. Doris did not behave though and as we crossed the North Sea, we heard reports of aircraft diverting, and having to go around because of wind shear warnings which are an instant NO. I was pilot flying and in the short amount of time we had, I briefed exactly what I was going to do if the landing couldn't be completed - we did this as a matter of course anyway, but today it was more meaningful. We worked out exactly what the wind strength would need to be for us to abandon the approach to stay within the crosswind limits, and as we started the approach, for the first and only time in my career, I was nervous. This was the strongest and gustiest crosswind I had ever landed in as a captain, and I had only experienced conditions like this on a handful of occasions as a first officer and I needed to get it right - granted I had a training captain sitting next to me but I had to discount that because he wouldn't always be there. I didn't let on that I was feeling anything other than confident that this was going to work, knowing I had many other plans up my sleeve, and as we started the final approach, I chose to ignore the devastation I could see below me that had been caused by this storm that had been raging for a couple of hours and was getting worse. Miraculously there was a lull as we came into land, and although the wind was strong, it was relatively smooth and the sense of relief that we were back on the ground was palpable. Glasgow was another story altogether.

By the time we had parked on the stand and unloaded and reloaded our passengers, the real storm was upon us. We could feel the wind rocking the aircraft as it pounded across the airfield gusting fifty-five and sometimes sixty knots (all speeds in aviation are measured in knots). We had boarded the passengers to try to go to Glasgow but as well as strengthening in speed, the wind had changed direction putting it firmly out of the aircraft's crosswind limits. All aircraft are limited to a maximum wind speed blowing at 90 degrees to the body of the aircraft - a crosswind - above which pilots are not permitted to take it into the air. This speed is lower for less experienced pilots, but my limit was the full 38knots across and we were well above that. The forecast was not in our favour and despite us joking to ourselves that we could give it a go (there are no old AND bold pilots remember) we knew that for us it was game over because we were rapidly running out of duty hours. The passengers remained on board and we called for backup which arrived in the form of Tariq who I had not seen for a few years - his hair was wild as he bounced onto the aircraft with his new crew and having said goodbye to our very patient passengers and handed everything over we made our way back to the crew room to debrief. It was without a doubt, the worst weather I have ever been airborne in and although I remained confident about my ability to operate to the maximum wind limits, I always thought twice about whether or not I was prepared to from then on.

There was a knock-on effect of this day ending earlier than we had planned, and that was that the check flights I should have completed on that day, had also been cut short, and so they had to be rescheduled. There were a couple of false starts when flights were scheduled and then dropped off the roster, but eventually, I was rostered another check flight day with another training captain, this time at Luton where I was based. We were to fly to Glasgow and back and then on to Berlin where there was a curfew. The Glasgow flight was great, but it was a busy time of year, and we picked up delays coming back into Luton that pushed us behind what was already a tight schedule, with another delay leaving Luton. We realised quite early on in the flight that we would just about manage to get into Berlin, but we would need a speedy turnaround on the ground to get away again before the night curfew was imposed. Pre-empting this, I decided to liaise with air traffic control and got the airport to agree that we could arrive and depart - there may not be time to load passenger bags, but we would at least get our passengers from Berlin back to London.

We were quite pleased with ourselves for co-ordinating this because it took quite a lot of effort, and then our faces fell as we received a message from the Operations department telling us that we would miss the curfew and that we must divert to Rostock and return empty from there. Our first reaction was to look at each other and say, "Where the actual fuck is Rostock?" We couldn't find it on any of our maps until we realised that because it is a half-military and half-civilian airport, it has a slightly different coding than we were looking for. It turned out that Rostock was miles from Berlin and since we had already co-ordinated our arrival and departure with Schoenefeld ATC we smugly replied to Ops saying, "Thank you very much but it's all sorted out, we have arranged to get into Berlin and out again" or words to that effect. The reply came back "Divert to Rostock." We had a decision to make, or rather I had a decision to make - because although I was flying with a training captain, it was my check ride and I had to make the decisions just as I would on a normal day. I weighed them up. I could pretend that I hadn't received the last message from the company and continue to Berlin, I could argue with them about the decision, or I could do as I was told and divert. I decided to start with gentle persuasion. "Are you sure - we have liaised with ATC." The reply was still the same and so, knowing that I was going to now have to confront 180 hacked-off passengers, I started programming the routing to Rostock... now that I knew where it was.

I had already told the passengers that we were having to divert, but I hadn't told them where, to spare the cabin crew a riot, and after shutting down the engines, and having received more information from the company, I went out to face the music. I explained what had happened, explained how the passenger's onward journey would be completed, and apologised profusely that we were not in Berlin, and I had barely managed to get the words out before the cabin erupted into the shouts of understandable angry Germans who had no option but to vent their fury at me. The coach journey would take more than 2 hours, by which time the trains into the city would have stopped running (like many airports, Berlin's main hub is not in the city itself but quite a long way away from the centre), and a taxi ride at that time of night would cost a lot of money. Tensions in the cabin started to escalate and the passengers were getting louder and louder and starting to leave their seats and head in my direction, and then they started calling me names in German - completely oblivious to the fact that I had been to school in Frankfurt, and studied German up to my first year at University - and I knew how to swear and what the word for whore was in German. They crossed a line. I had done my job to the best of my ability, and I would help them as much as I could - but they needed to remember to have some manners. My (very tall, rugby-playing) training captain appeared behind me ready to come to my aid as I spoke firmly down the address system. "You all need to SIT DOWN and STOP SHOUTING at me so that I can help you," I said, "and the most important part of that sentence is that you need to stop shouting!" They amazingly all sat down and stopped shouting immediately, and I added, "Also, you should know that I speak German fluently," this broke the mood completely as some people looked a bit shame-faced and others sniggered that I had known all along what they were saying. I spent the next hour answering people's questions, helping them to work out what they could do about their journeys and making sure everyone knew that we had tried everything we could to get them to Berlin. I had managed to win them over, saved a LOT of hassle from passengers whom I completely sympathised with, and I also learned later on from my cabin crew, that, when I get cross, I am quite scary - I suspect I learned this from having teenage children - I just wish they had been as compliant!

TALLIN - the one where I flew home with no trousers on

This story is not quite what you are thinking! Low cost is not the same thing as soft porn and there is a very stupid reason why this even happened in the first place.

From Stansted, we flew regularly to Tallinn in Estonia. It was quite a nice day out because it was a two-sector day (just there and back), took under four hours each way, and flying back down if the sun was in the right place, the Fresian Islands would give us spectacular views during an otherwise unremarkable flight.

It also felt a bit exotic flying to Tallinn - it is just so different from most of the other places we fly to for many reasons - firstly, it is still very reminiscent of everything I imagined an Eastern Bloc country to be - the architecture that is visible from the airport is very utilitarian, although I am told that it is a fantastic place to visit. Secondly, in winter, its runway is made entirely of snow - snow that is lit up in the same way as a normal runway, but snow nonetheless, and it is very cold. My airline had chosen not to take the option of providing foot heaters for the flight deck and so on these flights, especially in winter, our feet would be freezing by the time we arrived in Tallinn, so I always wore a pair of thick woolly tights underneath the cheap nylon of my uniform trousers, and thank goodness for that because, on this occasion, they proved to be something of a saviour.

I was flying with one of my favourite captains, he always called me Relish (he was from Sheffield, and there is a brand of sauce there called Henderson's Relish), and we had flown together often - most memorably until this flight, positioning an empty aircraft to Milans Linate airport and then travelling home via Copenhagen - a long but very funny day. It was my turn to fly the leg from Tallinn back to Stansted, and therefore as pilot flying, it was my responsibility to conduct the walk-around before the flight. This is slightly more than 'kicking the tyres' as we call it and is how we ensure that the aircraft is in good shape for each flight. When you see a pilot looking at the tyres, walking around the wings and checking inside the engines, they are carrying out this pre-flight check and this happens before every single flight. On this particular day (although it was winter and Tallinn is a long way north, so it was already dark) it was very cold and very snowy and the apron on which we were parked was covered in de-icing fluid from aircraft that had parked here earlier. I knew I needed to be careful and gingerly picked my way around the aircraft, careful to look up only if I was stationary. As I got back to the service steps up to the aircraft I grabbed hold of the handrail, just in time to feel the ground disappear from under my feet! I went down hard and landed not only on my hip but also in possibly the biggest puddle of sticky yellow de-icing fluid there could have been. It really hurt, and so did my pride - thank goodness it was dark so hopefully no one had seen me - I was also completely soaked.

I had been spotted by ground crew and they rushed over to make sure I was OK and helped me up - I was a bit bruised and soggy but otherwise I was fine, and I walked back into the flight deck to tell Captain Kev what had happened. Being the sympathetic group of people aircrew tend to be, we all laughed at my misfortune, and even more when we realised how much of me was covered in this yellow snot-like fluid. The big winter uniform coat I was wearing had protected me from the worst of it, but my trousers were drenched. There was no way I could sit in wet trousers for the next 3.5 hours, so I asked Kev how he would feel about me taking them off and drying them....again a burst of laughter and I made a joke about this being the way I chatted up all the best-looking captains of course and we decided it was the only sensible way for me to fly home. I did explain that I had thick tights on underneath and, they were so thick that they were more like leggings - and that was that - I flew back to Stansted with no trousers on. By the time we arrived, they had dried out which was very good news but not quite the end of the story. It had been snowing heavily in London and there had been lots of aircraft that had ended up diverting which meant they weren't in the right place. We had been asked if we would be willing to position our aircraft to Gatwick and taxi back to preserve as much as possible the integrity of the first wave from there the next morning. Being the company-minded, kind-spirited people we were, we had agreed - not completely altruistically - there is something very cool about flying an empty aircraft through a snowstorm at 7000ft down the eastern side of London, even if it is only an eighteen-minute flight!! We landed and sat like lemons for forty minutes waiting for information about a stand (no one had told them we were coming!) and finally made it into the crew room where we phoned Operations in Luton for details of our journey home. Captain Kev had been booked into a taxi home, and I had been booked into a hotel due to some nuanced duty limitation that I would breach if I took the taxi - there was NO WAY I was staying in a hotel in Gatwick with nothing but trousers covered in the now dried but nasty de-icing fluid to wear for the next 24 hours. I didn't even need to put my foot down on this - Kev stepped in like a Knight in shining armour - or at least, a captain in nylon uniform, and explained in no uncertain terms that we would both be going back in the taxi. It worked, there was paperwork involved but we set off together, around an M25 that was reduced to one lane due to the snow, with possibly the fastest, rally car taxi driver in the world - we thought we might die at one point until Kev politely but firmly asked him to, "Slow down mate, we've got all night!"

We did make it back to Stansted intact, and despite the hair-raising journey we were still laughing as we said goodbye, and we are still friends to this day - I just hope that Kev's wife knew about the no trousers story before now!

Chapter Twelve

Flying without Wings

It is a Monday evening at the end of July 2021, and I have just arrived back in Inverness after a whistle-stop tour to London which has been a momentous and eventful 24 hours. It is momentous only because of the time that has passed since the last time I flew to London and back, and it is eventful because as I always used to, I have crammed so much in - and I am tired and pleased to be home as I walk down the steps of the aircraft and into the terminal building.

I am on the phone with Rich who is my right-hand man at Wingman, and who has run our mobile lounge project since its inception. We are discussing the launch of Bus 2 which we have decided to name Wingbee. It will launch at East Grinstead on Monday 26th July and Rich is asking me if I can be there for the launch as a surprise for the volunteers. I pause to think about this for a minute - it has been more than a year since I have been in London, and I have only left Moray a handful of times - I don't know if I want to fly, be in a big city, be away from home - but I also haven't been south to visit any of the Wingman lounges (except travelling to Edinburgh for the closing of that lounge a year ago), I haven't seen either of the busses, and although I have worked closely with him for the last 16 months, and we have become good friends, I also haven't met Rich face to face. My diary is pretty clear and there are cheap flights available so I decide that I am going to go. I want to be there for the launch of the bus, and I think it will be good to show my face to some of the crew. I also think it will be good for me to see firsthand, the work that we have been doing and all that we have achieved. It is easy to get lost in the day-to-day running of a charity that has become as large as ours has over the last few months and sometimes the awesomeness of everything that we HAVE done gets lost as we wade our way through problem-solving, fundraising, crewing and governance.

Five minutes later, my flights are booked, I have arranged to stay overnight with my son in Lewisham, and Rich and I have agreed that we will keep my visit a secret so we can surprise people. I find myself looking forward to it which is a surprise as I have become very comfortable staying at home in my little bubble.

I feel it is safe to travel - aircraft are being cleaned perhaps better than they ever have before, I have had both my vaccinations, England is opening up and Scotland is not far behind. Plus, I will be in control of where I am all the time and as a self-confessed control freak (and proud of it!) I am much more comfortable doing something familiar even if I haven't done it for a long time. The added bonus is that I will get to see Tom who went to University in London five years ago and has never moved home.

As the date gets nearer it becomes harder and harder to keep my visit a secret - we are advertising the launch of the bus and people keep asking if I am going to be there - I finally crack on the Friday before and tell one or two people who won't be there but this is actually for practical reasons as I need to get to the Hospital once I arrive in East Grinstead and I also need to get back to Luton afterwards to fly home. Although I am looking forward to it, I am also a little bit nervous about flying again for the first time in 16 months, and how it will feel to once again be sitting on an aircraft I not only used to fly, but was in charge of, but now as a regular passenger. I think my biggest worry is that I will step on board the aircraft and realise that not only have I made the biggest mistake of my life in leaving but knowing that there is currently no way back and is unlikely to be for enough years that it will be too late. Even a Hobson's choice is better than no choice at all and I don't sleep very much the night before - when I do, my dreams are even more strange than usual - and I do have a lot of strange dreams!

Jim drives me to the airport in our little TT (which I have always pretended is an Aston Martin on the inside) and as he knows I am quite emotional about making this journey, he tells me that he will make sure he calls out, "See you tomorrow," if I cry as I walk into the terminal. This makes us both laugh because I have a habit of crying in airports. Years ago, when I was still a teenager, I dropped my dad off at Heathrow; he did a lot of business in America and went away quite a lot. I used to enjoy dropping him off and picking him up because, in those pre-mobile phone days, it meant I got two hours each way of his undivided attention and even better, his jokes. On this occasion, I went into the terminal with him to wave him off through security, and as I always did, I cried as we said goodbye, standing and waving until he disappeared.

Standing nearby were two armed policemen, and seeing how sad I was they came over to ask if I was ok, presumably thinking I must have been waving my dad off for a long time, they tried hard to hide their mirth when my dad turned around and called, "See you on Friday," it was a Monday afternoon but I could see them smirking through their concerned looks and decided it was kinder to join them and explain that I always cry saying goodbye to my dad but that I was grateful to them for caring anyway. I am sure they thought I was bonkers which was just fine with me because it was quite nice to have the attention of armed and uniformed police officers even if they were quietly giggling as I turned and walked back to the car. It has been a standing joke in my (cruel) family ever since and one that Jim likes to dine out on whenever possible. He is out of luck this afternoon however as he has made me laugh as I head off into the terminal.

The first thing that is different is wearing a mask - like everyone else, I have worn mine whenever I have been inside but we don't go anywhere much inside where we live so it is not something I am used to - and now that I am in the terminal, I must keep the mask on until I step outside the terminal at Luton. Despite the mask, the staff in security recognise me from the many times I have been through the airport in the past both as a passenger and as operating crew, and it is good to see them, even though it is hard having to explain to them that I am no longer working and that they won't be seeing me in uniform any more. I find an empty seat look out at the apron and wait for my flight to arrive, and as I do I realise that I hadn't prepared myself for how strange it would be to be back in a place I am so familiar with but without any of the trappings that go with that orange lanyard and ID card - the front door of an Airbus is not the only door that opens in an airport when you have crew ID! It takes me by surprise how emotional I am to be flying again after so long but not being part of the machinery. As I watch G-UZHI pull on to stand I am embarrassed to once again be sitting in an airport with tears rolling down my face and soaking into my mask. I can't even wear my sunglasses because by now, anyone who does not know that it's impossible to wear a mask AND any type of glasses at the same time must have been living under a stone for the previous sixteen months or have excellent eyesight and live somewhere really dark!

I have to pull myself together. I can't board an aircraft in tears and although I would normally say hello to the crew and enjoy some time talking with them, this time I want to just hide in my seat and be alone with my thoughts. It feels really good to get close to 'my' aircraft again, and very unusually for me, I board at the back, find my seat, plug my headphones in and turn the music up loud for the entire flight. It passes quickly and I roll my eyes as the wheels make firm contact with the runway (like every landing I ever made was smooth for goodness sake!). I loved working in Luton and made lots of friends there but as I walked through the posh new terminal building, I was struck that even this level of change did not make me love the airport any more than I used to - it was the people who made those four years so good. I find the bus to the train station and settle into a quiet journey into London, I will arrive in plenty of time for dinner and have some things to do on the way.

Of course, it can't be this easy. Almost an hour later, the train is still sitting in the station at Harpenden and eventually the reason for this is announced. There are pedestrians on the track further down the line and we are going nowhere fast. Great - we have dinner reservations in less than two hours, and I need to get to Lewisham. The trump card I have up my sleeve is that we spent two fantastic years living not too far away in Bushey Heath and because of that, I know that if I can get to Stanmore, I can get the Jubilee Line around to London Bridge and then switch for Lewisham. Uber is my friend and as I leave the station, I say to a group of strangers who are milling around that if anyone wants to join me they will be more than welcome. One man steps forward who needs to get back to Greenwich and we set off feeling smug that we have beaten the delays and should still get to where we need to be on time.

During the journey, we find out a little bit more about each other, and by some crazy stroke of chance, we discover we have a very funny and very good mutual friend - in fact, we have several mutual friends which is almost too much of a coincidence, and by the time we say goodbye at London Bridge we have swapped details and promised to keep in touch - now I appreciate that in 2021, when no one talks to anyone else on the tube or anywhere else, this must sound strange, but it does make me wonder about the missed opportunities that are wasted by people keeping their heads down, their AirPods in, and shut themselves off completely from the rest of the world - yes, I am that annoying person who goes to the bright lights of the big city and dares to be friendly to everyone - and I'm proud of it!

Arriving in Lewisham just in time, I am excited to see Tom and his girlfriend, and we have a lovely meal before they show me around their new flat where I am spending the night, I am impressed by the amazing views of London from the roof garden.

I am up early the next morning as I need to catch a train to Horley where I am being collected by Carey, another member of the Wingman Management Team, and another new friend. I have met Carey before as he recently stayed with us in Scotland, so it is nice to see a familiar face and we have a chance to talk shop on our way to the hospital. As we turn the corner into the hospital car park, I see Wingbee, our bus, for the first time and although I have seen photos, I am impressed by how completely amazing it looks in its blue and white Project Wingman livery, complete with stripey awning, green astroturf outside, deckchairs, and a white picket fence. It is amazing and it represents almost a year of really hard work, finding a suitable bus, and finding ways to fundraise (we set a target of £100,000 to crowdfund in the run-up to Christmas and although the actual crowdfunding fell short we managed to raise the money in other ways not just for our first bus - Wellbee, but now for our second), planning what the buses would look like on the inside and out, working out where they would go, how we would crew them, hours and hours of meetings and decisions, and taking massive leaps of faith, and sitting in front of me is the result - and it is stunning. Being new, it is a shiny bus anyway, but as with Wellbee, we have raised the roof, which is now perspex, and filled the top deck with as many removable seats as COVID restrictions will allow, making the most of the already fitted kitchen and seating area downstairs. We have - or more accurately Rich has - become bus conversion experts of sorts and I am so amazed and proud to now be standing before this brilliant bus, saying hello to our brilliant volunteers who proudly put on their uniforms every day from whichever airline they work for (or our own if they no longer have one) so that they can spend another day offering tea and empathy to NHS staff. It is an incredible achievement and I get first-hand experience of what Project Wingman means to people throughout the day when volunteers and NHS staff alike, take time to tell me what a difference everything we have been doing has made to their own lives. More than one person has told me that Project Wingman has saved their lives over the last sixteen months, and I am as proud of this as I am sad for the fact it has become necessary in the first place. There is an official opening ceremony when the Chair of the Board of Trustees cuts a blue ribbon and makes a lovely speech, followed by me - an opportunity for me to say thank you to everyone for everything they have done to make this possible. Sometime in the afternoon, I have an opportunity to experience firsthand why our charity is so important and what an impact we can have on the lives of people who need us. A lady approaches me and asks me what the bus is there for and what we are doing. I explain, and she asks if it is just for NHS staff, so I tell her that it is predominantly for NHS staff but that we would never turn anyone away who was in need. She asks me if I have

5 minutes to talk, and we find somewhere private. She tells me that she is waiting for her husband but that her father recently suffered a stroke, and as he lives overseas with the rest of her family, she has only been able to visit once and was shocked at the state she found him in. She won't be able to see him again and wishes she could stop him from suffering. The pain in her eyes is almost tangible and all she needs is for someone to listen. This is the value of being able to talk to someone you don't know, and this is exactly what we set out to do in the beginning. After almost an hour, she has to go and collect her husband, but she tells me she feels a lot better for having been able to share her worries with someone, thanks me for being there and leaves. I don't know the lady's name or anything else about her, and I don't need to. I am left feeling humbled that I have been able to play a small part in making someone else's day less difficult and it reminds me why we are doing this in the first place.

The rest of the day is a blur of welcoming NHS staff, speaking to the volunteers, taking photos, making promotional videos, and crucially, eating cake, and it is soon time to leave. I am getting a lift to Luton with Esther who has been my friend for fifteen years and is one of our directors. Esther and I met when we were both flying instructors in High Wycombe and I was one of the instructors who taught the man who would become Esther's husband to fly. During the first week of setting up Project Wingman we very quickly reached a point where we had so many people signing up to help that I could not manage it all on my own and having recently lost her job when regional airline FlyBe collapsed, Esther offered to help. She was the first person to come onboard and very quickly got my pathetic attempt at a spreadsheet into order as well as becoming a valuable and wise ally as the charity grew and changed shape. Having each other's undivided attention on the two-hour drive to Luton was one of life's rare gifts and we arrived back at Luton in plenty of time for my flight home.

The last time I flew out of Luton was the day I flew home just before lockdown, and it was desolate. I had never seen such a sad and lonely-looking place, and although not empty this time, the terminal was still a shadow of its former self with only a handful of passengers waiting for flights, no queues at security and happily for me, the lounge was still open. Sadly, for them, I was only the third customer of the day, and since the wine I had asked for was out of stock, the lovely staff decided instead to offer me a glass of Prosecco which was a perfect way to finish such a busy and exciting day.

I was much less emotional on the flight home, and boarding at the front this time, was delighted to see two familiar faces on the flight deck, one of whom was a friend from Stansted days, and the other of whom had been instrumental in getting me through my failed attempt at command and my return to the right-hand seat. It was so good to see them and stepping into the flight deck for the first time in sixteen months, I was expecting to feel a pull back into the captain's seat, and a need to return to the skies... this time I was prepared - so when nothing happened I was amazed. Surely after 8500 hours of flying around in this tiny office with amazing views, I would want to return to it once again -

but nothing at all. We exchanged bits of news, and I took my seat in the cabin for the flight home.

There were many reasons why I chose to accept voluntary redundancy in September 2020, and I still believe it was Hobson's choice that without COVID, I would never have made. One of the reasons though was training in the simulator. I hated it. There were rare occasions when I came out of a simulator session feeling like I could rule the world, but mostly I left my six-monthly check ride thinking, 'Thank goodness that's over', and the longer I spent on the ground last year, the more this 'sim fear' built up. If I were to return to flying now, I would have to spend a LOT of time in the simulator and I have zero desire to do that. I loved the job I did, but it has changed almost beyond recognition in many ways and standing in the flight deck on this day has reaffirmed my thinking that I have a heart full of gratitude for the 12 years I spent sitting at the front of a passenger jet, flying around Europe, I have done that now and I don't need to go back and do it again. I have amazing memories, and made wonderful friends, and without those years at Stansted, Lyon, Luton, Porto and Gatwick, I would never have been able to rustle up the support I needed to make Project Wingman a reality, and the difference we have collectively made to the lives of NHS Staff and Aircrew alike would never have been possible.

Landing in Inverness feels like a homecoming that was meant to be, and having said goodbye to the crew, I walk down the ramp onto the apron, turn back to wave one last time to my friends on board, and walk into the terminal without looking back. I have operated into this airport more times than I can think of, in good weather and bad, finding gaps in fog to get my passengers home on days when no other aircraft has managed it, landing in crosswinds that have made me proud of a job well done, on nights that are light all night long, and in the middle of winter when it barely gets light at all. I have flown my dad to work in London and home again, I have flown my son and one of my daughters, I have flown friends, I have made friends with people who have been regular passengers, always making my welcome on board announcements from the front of the cabin, keeping my passengers as informed as my crew, and building my professional reputation on making people feel like the priority I believe they should be. I have celebrated Hogmanay, birthdays, and wedding anniversaries on board these aircraft for 12 years and spent almost an entire year in the sky, and as I walk out of the terminal into a sunny July evening, to find Jim waiting in our sporty little TT, I know that I have made the right decisions for the right reasons, and everything that has gone before was worthwhile.

There are so many things that have had to come together over so many years for any of this to make sense and this is what I am thinking as I walk out of the terminal towards the car park. If I hadn't met and subsequently been spectacularly dumped by a boy I thought I loved at the age of 18 (we have all been there right?) I would never have ended up choosing Leeds as the place I wanted to study. If I hadn't walked through freshers fair and seen the gigantic sign saying, 'Learn to fly for free', I would never have applied for and subsequently gained a place on the Yorkshire University Air Squadron, and if I hadn't joined that, I would never have been in the Officers Mess bar at RAF Finningley at the right moment to meet my husband. Leaving the UK in 2003 for an exchange tour in New Zealand seemed crazy at the time as we had only been in our house for a year and assumed we would stay there forever... but that posting changed our lives in so many ways - on a very personal level it allowed me to find out who I am away from the comfort of everything I knew, and also gave me a much better appreciation of the merits of a Marlborough Sauvignon Blanc versus say a Wairarapa Chardonnay - much more buttery! - this is an essential life skill and one which has served me well at every bar and restaurant I have ever been to since... New Zealand was also pivotal though because it was where my flying training continued and therefore the beginning of a journey through a career in which I made and still have so many friends around the world. They are not all pilots anymore either, but that's ok. The Da Vinci quote says, 'Once you have tasted flight, you will forever walk the earth with your eyes turned skyward, for there you have been, and there you will always long to return.' It is true but that does not mean there is a need for every pilot to spend the rest of their lives in the flight deck or even in the air. So many of these people have taught me the value of understanding that sometimes the season passes and something else comes along. Our friend Andy, having left the RAF and moved his whole family to New Zealand to start a new career in the RNZAF was then diagnosed with type one diabetes which cost him his medical and subsequently his job. We visited them when we returned to New Zealand in 2007 expecting him to be very downbeat about what had happened only to find that he was completely the opposite and his words have stuck with me. "I have spent the last eighteen years flying planes for a living, now I will just have to find a proper job," he said in his broad Glaswegian accent and with a big smile on his face. He knew that he had been one of the lucky ones for so many years and he graciously accepted that sometimes things change, and we must embrace that - preferably with a large and cold glass of Savvy!

Returning to the UK as a qualified pilot meant that I met people during my licence conversion and subsequent instructor rating who have been instrumental in the building and running of Project Wingman - and whilst the initial connection is important, keeping relationships going over years and multiple moves has been equally important. Some of this has been about paying it forward. I was lucky to be awarded a scholarship for my instructor rating and I always vowed that somehow I would repay this even if not financially. I have done this with Project Wingman by providing a safe place to fall for aircrew during the most challenging times we have ever seen, but also by all the school visits and mentoring of young pilots, I have done over the years and continue to do. And finally, the twelve incredible years I spent at easyJet, firstly as a Senior First Officer and then as a Captain, working at 5 different bases in the UK and Europe, meeting so many amazing people and practising everything I have always believed about how to treat people, I firmly believe that was fundamental to the setting up and success of a charity that has not only helped the NHS but thousands of aircrew throughout the UK and hopefully will continue to do this into the future. Things happen for reasons we often can't see at the time, whether good or challenging and the secret is to grab every opportunity with an open mind, and open arms and live each day as if it is the last we will ever have because life can turn on a pin, and as I discovered first hand, we can't ever take tomorrow for granted. It is almost always with the benefit of hindsight that we see the reasons for these things, and I am in no doubt at all that this season too will pass, and whatever the future holds will be an adventure worth taking.

I will fly many more times as a passenger, and because none of us know what the future holds, and because life can turn on a pin, I don't know if I will ever step back in the flight deck again, but as we drive home and I explain to Jim that I know that a season has passed, he rolls his eyes, smiles and tells me that's ok, which sums up the reason I have been able to do any of it at all. We are about to celebrate our 26th wedding anniversary, and for all of those years and more he has been my Wingman, the wind beneath my wings, my champion and I know that whatever comes next will not only be ok, but a journey worth taking, because everything up to now has given us a wonderful life that we have been able to share with wonderful people, we have been weathered by the seasons, been battered by storms, enjoyed moments of calm, and somehow found ways. through it all, and everything has found its place.

Chapter Thirteen

Keep Calm and Fly On

Despite our best efforts, sometimes things happen when we are flying that we can't plan for...

One of those things is bird activity. Airfields are really attractive places for birds - they are large open spaces with no people around and the occasional irritating aircraft which is limited to a small strip of tarmac running down the middle - if I were a bird, I would be interested in setting up home in one of these places.

This is managed well by airports - the grass is kept short to discourage birds from nesting, and bird control measures are in place to make it as safe an operating environment as possible - and whilst we can control what machines operate in the skies and where, we can't do the same for birds - they were here first after all! Throughout my career, I have had very few encounters with birds, but when I have, it has been thought-provoking, to say the least, if not trouser-changing on the odd occasion.

There was the birdstrike in Palma which caused a four-hour delay because when a bird hits an aircraft (or an aircraft hits a bird depending on your viewpoint) engineering checks have to be carried out to certify that the aircraft is safe to operate - especially if it makes a dent in the leading edge of a wing - in this case, the dent was inspected and deemed to be safe - but that decision has to be made by a certified engineer who is qualified on that particular aircraft type, and is way beyond the remit of a pilot to decide.

And then there was a similar event on an aircraft which I was booked to travel on as a passenger on my days off which caused an even longer delay - I was collecting my children from boarding school for the half-term holidays and we were happily sitting with another family in the departure lounge at Inverness, excited to have the children home for a week. The aircraft arrived and we all got ourselves ready to be called for boarding, but the call didn't come. Uh oh, I thought jumping straight on to my company intranet to see if I could find out what had happened - or at least find out what sort of delay we could expect - the answer wasn't encouraging.

This was one of the defining moments of my career too actually because what happened next kept 180 passengers completely on side and even though the eventual delay was something in the region of 6 hours, everyone was happy because they had information - I decided on that day that this was the captain I was going to be when the time came.

The captain came into the terminal and made an announcement over the PA explaining that evidence of a bird strike had been found on the wing and that this needed to be inspected. At that time engineering support was only available in Glasgow or Aberdeen and the Aberdeen engineer was not available. This was not going to be a quick fix.

I spoke to the captain and showed him my ID and explained that I was a First Officer based at Stansted and if there was anything I could do to help him on the inside of the terminal while he was on the aircraft waiting, I would be happy to help.

Time passed, the kids were remarkably chilled out, and eventually, another aircraft was summoned from London to 'rescue' everyone. It was a race to see who would arrive first, the engineer or the new aircraft.

The new aircraft won the race, and the captain asked me to help him set it all up for departure while he handed over the original aircraft to the incoming crew - we eventually made it home 6 hours later than planned but were happy because we had felt all along that we had been well looked after and well informed - it was a win

Then there was the unfortunate bird that was flying in the same place as the captain's windshield on the way into Copenhagen at 8000ft and 250 knots. The impression left on the heated windscreen was the perfect shape of a hawk meaning that I had to take over operating the rest of the flight because I could see out of my side! The passengers didn't even know that this had happened - they didn't need to - but it caused a delay because we had to clean the bird off the windshield before we could leave Copenhagen - it wasn't a pretty task and for reasons known only to the engineers in Copenhagen, one that was left to us as crew - it turns out that the plastic cutlery given to us in our onboard catering packs worked ok with bottles of water but we weren't exactly overjoyed to have had to carry this out ourselves.

My only experience of a bird strike as a captain was on a flight out of Corfu. It was a beautiful day and Corfu is somewhere that I always loved flying to - the approach is interesting enough to make you think about it and on this particular runway, you come into land over the bridge that connects the airport to Corfu Town. We had made up a little bit of time on the way down and we were leaving on time to go home - it was all going well.

I was operating as the 'Pilot Flying' and as always there was that sense of anticipation as I lined my fully loaded A320 up on the runway. We received our take-off clearance, I set the thrust levers to 50% thrust to ensure the engines spooled up evenly, then the setting known as TOGA, for Take Off Go Around, and we started to roll down the runway. At around 140mph, I gently pulled back on the control column to lift the aircraft nose off the runway and we were airborne, and there it was - right in front of us as we climbed through about one hundred feet, a big white bird which we saw only briefly before we heard a loud BANG somewhere on the fuselage we thought - bugger - a birdstrike on take-off - not good. We weren't sure where the bird had hit the aircraft, but we needed more than anything else to just fly - get the aircraft away from the ground and to an altitude where we could safely decide about what to do next. We gingerly raised the gear, not sure if the body of the bird had hit the nose wheel and become wedged, and everything worked ok. We spoke to the cabin crew who confirmed that everyone on board had heard the bang and several passengers sitting on the right-hand side of the aircraft had seen a puff of smoke coming out of the right engine as the fan blades and 720degree heat of the exhaust gases turned it into pink mist. Bird in the engine - ok, the aircraft is still operating normally, and all the engine indications look normal - by now we have cleaned up the aircraft which means retracting the flaps we extend on the wing to create more lift, and we are climbing away from Corfu on our planned routing, having reported the birdstrike to the airport in case some of it is left on the runway. We have plenty of options, the aircraft is running as I would expect it to, Italy is off the nose to the left and there are multiple airports we can easily land at on our route back to Gatwick. We discuss the options as we are trained to do, and it is a pretty simple decision to continue with our route back to London where the aircraft is expected to be and where we have a large team of engineers. If anything should happen on the way, we can divert.

I speak to the passengers to explain what has happened and reassure them that everything is just as it should be, and we arrive back at Gatwick, not only in one piece but early.

Once the passengers have departed, I meet the engineer who is already inspecting the engine. All that is left of the bird is a smear of blood on the inside of the engine nacelle (the front bit of the engine intake), and the revolting smell of an entire (reasonably large) bird being simultaneously cooked and shredded. Not a happy ending for the bird which we were later informed was an Egret. I looked it up and was surprised to find how large it was - no wonder it made a bang!!

Bird strikes don't happen that often though, and I suspect if you are reading this book, you are also likely to have either watched the movie 'Miracle on the Hudson' with Tom Hanks coolly playing the role of Captain Chesley Sullenberger or Sully as he was known, safely landing an airbus on the Hudson River in New

York having flown through a large flock of migrating geese and losing both engines at the same time - this happens rarely, and when you think of the number of aircraft that take off every hour of every day, it just shows what a safe working environment we do enjoy as pilots.

We can't control birds any more than we can control the weather, and knowing as much as we can about the weather becomes something of an obsession for pilots. We monitor it and watch it and try and understand it ALL the time - when I wake up in the morning, the first thing I check is the weather where I am, and the forecast weather for where I am going - firstly, is it going to be raining when I get to work because I hate doing the walk round in the rain and being slightly soggy in the flight deck - it's not a nice feeling at all!

Will there be strong winds today - not a problem for us as pilots, but it might make it turbulent for the passengers, will there be no wind today - more of a problem for us because it might mean fog, especially if we are landing near water, or will it be so hot that I will need to run the small engine at the back of the aircraft called an Auxiliary Power Unit or APU for the length of the turnaround - and if so, do I have a working APU today (they go wrong more than you would think - which is why it is a good thing that they are 'auxiliary'!), or will it be so cold that I will need to de-ice the aircraft before we take off. There is always something - and sometimes that something is fog.

Not long after I got command I was operating a flight to Lisbon which at our scheduled take-off time was operating in Low Visibility which meant a sea fog had rolled in from the Atlantic and all aircraft were having to land using the automatic landing systems installed at each end of the runway. Whilst this meant flights were still able to operate, it requires a much, much, MUCH greater distance between landing aircraft and slows everything down so much that it creates delays. In our case, a four-hour delay. The fog was forecast to clear, and we expected the restriction to come forward, so we boarded the passengers and left our stand on time. We then taxied round to the compass testing bay near the runway at Luton where we positioned ourselves nose out for when it was time to go, shut down our engines and invited passengers into the flight deck to have a small glimpse into our world. I always did this during a delay if there was time - it does several things - it passes the time more quickly for everyone on board, and it cheers passengers up no end when they realise that even though they won't arrive on time, they will have sat in the hallowed captain's seat of a passenger aircraft and lived out one of their childhood dreams if only for a moment - you would be surprised at the number of people who decide to take us up on this offer! The other thing this achieves is that it allows me to gauge the mood of the passengers and support the cabin crew in their mission to look after everyone on board. We hand out free water and I usually offer to carry this up and down the cabin to all the passengers, talking to them as I go - I enjoy this immensely, I love meeting the people I am flying with and finding out a little bit about the reasons they are travelling! I also make sure that even if there is nothing new to say, I update the passengers regularly about our delay. It turns out that even if there is no news, people don't like to feel as if they are forgotten, and like to feel as if someone is doing their best to look after them!

Eventually, it is our time to leave Luton and as we make our way down through the South of England, over the Brest Peninsula and into the Bay of Biscay we are surprised that the fog is not lifting as we were told it would. We set up the aircraft and brief for an automatic landing - and no, this is not the usual way of landing an aircraft. Ordinarily, it is the pilots who land the aircraft - and it is always the landings on which we grade our performance!! When it is foggy though, we have no option but to allow the aircraft to land itself using the instrumentation on board and the equipment on the ground to not only land automatically but to continue in a straight line on landing until we disconnect the autopilot at a slow enough speed. If you have ever sat at the front of an aircraft and heard a chirping sound after the aircraft has landed, that has been an automatic landing. It is the only occasion when all electronic devices on board have to be switched fully off as well so the chances are you will already know when it is going to happen.

We are fully expecting to autoland down to Lisbon, and just before we start the approach we notice that the wind has picked up a little and the fog is starting to clear - very quickly. By the time we turn onto our final approach track, the fog has all but disappeared and it is a gin clear day - no need for autoland anymore, so I disconnect the autopilot and fly the rest of the approach myself and after we have parked on the stand I do a quick departure announcement thanking everyone for their patience and promising them that there honestly was thick fog until about 20 minutes ago - they smile as they leave the aircraft into the now warm and sunny day but I am not sure that everyone completely believed me!

There is another place I fly to often which has a propensity to suffer from fog - and that is Inverness, my local airport and one I always have a vested interest in landing at because I often know many of the passengers, and also, I get to go home for a night! Unlike Lisbon however, Inverness does not have an automatic landing system installed which means that when the fog rolls in, all flights have to stop. Sometimes it clears, sometimes it sits for days, and sometimes it can clear a little bit in the middle of the day only to roll back in later. It is fickle and not easily predictable but if there is one place I can go to try and find out what is possible, it is the amazing Aberdeen MET office which I now have the phone number for safely stored on my iPhone. One typical winter day, the fog is so thick in Inverness that it isn't worth pushing back from our stand - it is far better to wait on the ground than it is to burn fuel in the air going round and round the hold hoping for something to change - some of my passengers have already chosen not to travel as they are not expecting me to be able to get into Inverness but I have promised the rest of them that I will do everything I can to land there today. I call Aberdeen and ask them what the chances are - they reckon there will be about a 45-minute window of opportunity so I organise with Gatwick that I will be able to push back from my stand and take off at a time that fits in with this window. I have plenty of fuel on board just in case but up to Inverness, the weather reports stay the same - there is no change. We decide to give it a go anyway on the basis that we can always perform a go-around and divert to Aberdeen if we need to - and miraculously - just as the Aberdeen MET office predicted, the fog starts to clear just as we are making our final descent into my home airport. By the time we are on finals, it is still a little bit hazy but more than good enough for us to make our approach and land the aircraft ourselves. We are the only aircraft to arrive that day and the fog closes in around us not long after we arrive - but we got there, and our passengers were grateful that day - years later, people I know who were on the flight still talk about it to me - there was a lot of luck involved but also a bit of local knowledge goes a long way!

Chapter Fourteen

A Royal Approach

It is still light as I join the back of a long queue that snakes from the towering West Door of Britain's Coronation Cathedral, down the scaffolding-clad side, past the North Doorway and St Margarets Church, out through a guarded gate which opens onto Abingdon Street and back on to Parliament Square and the Broad Sanctuary which is where we have arrived, giddy with the thought of what is about to happen, and in my case, marvelling at how lovely London always looks at this time of day regardless of whether or not it is almost Christmas.

As I look towards Parliament Square, my mind jumps back thirty years to a time when I lobbied Parliament to put pressure on the South African government to release Nelson Mandela. His statue now stands across the other side of the square from the Palace of Westminster and I feel a sense of pride that even then, at eighteen years old, I was brave enough to stand up for what I believed in.

As we chat excitedly, moving slowly forward with the queue, others join behind us and although I am really happy to be here, I can't wait to sit down. My feet (thanks to some cheap boots and a late night out in Mayfair the night before) are in agony - not feet, one of them is fine, the other however boasts blisters the size of small villages on the ball - and for the second day in a row, I have committed the cardinal sin of wearing heels in London despite knowing from years of either living here or visiting, that the ONLY shoes anyone should ever wear in London are flats, preferably trainers, and even better, crocs. It is not until you are wearing heels that you realise how completely uneven the streets of London are. The ones that aren't cobbled are far from smooth - it must be a nightmare for anyone who has to use sticks to get around, and as comfortable as Crocs would be right now, they just wouldn't do this afternoon.

We notice that everyone around us has yellow tickets instead of our green ones and start to wonder if we have come to the wrong entrance, but no, we are reassured that the colour of the tickets just helps them to know where we are to be seated.

Of course, it is Covid times and so we have all to show proof of a negative lateral flow test done this morning, and this, as well as our ticket and ID, is checked before we are even allowed into the grounds of this vast cathedral in which we will soon blissfully be sitting.

Earlier in the day I travelled from my brother in laws house in Clapham where my daughter has been working as a nanny to our nephews, to meet my parents who are staying at the Tower Hotel for a week to celebrate their Golden Wedding earlier in the year. It is on this journey, and too late to turn back to change into something else, that I realise that my feet are battered from the night before, and so I hobble from Tower Hill to the Hotel, check the damage in my parents hotel room and then hobble to a coffee shop looking over St Katherines Dock - it is like a tourists day out as my next stop after leaving my daughter to go for lunch in the city with my parents, is the OXO Tower where I meet my friend and colleague Rich for lunch. It is delicious and lunch with a view, as well as being such precious face-to-face time after months of Zoom and phone calls. Over the last two years, Rich has become one of my closest friends as we have navigated our way through the challenges that have been thrown at us whether of our own making or not. Lunch for me is Sea Bass - delicious with the hair of the dog New Zealand Sauvignon Blanc I was hoping Rich would choose to go with it, and we catch up on the last few weeks and discuss plans for 2022 while we eat. When it is time to leave I confess that there is no way I will be able to walk to the restaurant where we are meeting the rest of our group - ordinarily, this wouldn't be a problem but today it's a taxi day and I am impressed that on asking the reception if they had a number for a cab, they not only called one but have it waiting downstairs for us when we got there!

By the time we reach the end of the queue, we have picked up Zoe, another of my dear friends and colleagues, Rowan and Jack who I have got to know more recently. Rowan has travelled from Birmingham, Jack from Manchester, Zoe from Bristol and Rich from Yeovil (via Milton Keynes which is another story), and because we live all over the country, and I live way up north on the Moray Firth, we rarely get to have face to face meetings and it always strikes me when I have a live meeting with one of my team how tall they all are! I have known Zoe for years and met Rich a few times before, but Rowan and Jack are new to me in the flesh but also so familiar from the neck upwards! These times are strange, and it has made us all see things differently and also made us extremely grateful that today is happening at all when so much is being cancelled again. For months we have been getting used to uncertainty based on a known thing - what is called the Delta variant of this virus that has shut the world down for the last two years and changed all our lives completely and indefinitely. What we are now starting to face is a new wave that is named Omicron (it is working its way through the Greek alphabet faster than most people including me can recite it!) - it is now uncertainty based on more uncertainty and the airline industry, of which we are all a part, is being repeatedly hammered. Whilst the other three are all still working, Rowan and I, both captains at different airlines are no longer flying, I through the choice of voluntary redundancy, Rowan because the airline she worked for - Flybe - collapsed shortly before the crisis officially began. It is this aviation link, as well as the common ground of running the charity we have been eating, living and breathing since March 2020, that gives us the familiarity of people who have known each other for much longer than the twenty months it has been since we all met, and as we make our way down the side of the Abbey, through the security screening we are all so familiar with, and towards the West Door through which we will enter, we feel the excitement building the closer we get.

Just as we near the front of the queue, the gates are closed - are we too late we wonder? Have we been locked out? There are still a lot of people behind us so that can't be it - and then we see them - two Police cars leading a cavalcade with the Royal State

Bentley in the middle which stops immediately outside the West Door of the Abbey - flash guns light up the sky which has by now, turned a deep, inky blue, and Princess Catherine, joined by her husband Prince William have arrived at the Abbey to be greeted by a choir of children singing Christmas carols, and two reindeer who are visiting for the occasion and drawing almost as much attention as the Prince and Princess!

Finally, the gate is opened again, and we make our way into the Abbey, stopping to admire the reindeer as we go, and joking with the Press photographers as we pass them too. You can't help but look up in total awe as you pass through the West Door - the scale of this Cathedral is vast, and as I walk up the steps and into the Abbey, I look up into the eyes of Princess Catherine herself - she is as lovely and perfect in the flesh as she is on screen and in the magazines, and when I smile and say hello, I am slightly star-struck to find that she smiles and says hello back - for one brief moment, we are just two people greeting each other, and then the moment is gone as she returns to being a well-loved Princess and I am ushered off to the left-hand side of the nave to find my seat. We walk past rows of people who are already seated, past the wooden crib, and to the back of the choir, and I comment to Zoe that it is a shame to be sitting so far down as we may not see anything - and then we find our seats, in the North Transept with its Statesmen's Aisle, lined with marble statues of former Prime Ministers - we are sitting with a larger than life, marble version of William Gladstone peering down at us as he has done for over 100 years.

Our seats have giant plastic candles on them, and we instantly try and switch them on - disappointed to find that they appear to be broken - an usher tells us that they were also used at a Spice Girls concert - were they broken then too we wonder? Four out of the five of us are pilots, and we can't help ourselves - we have to start looking at the bottom of the candles to see if we can 'fix' them - surely there must be something wrong with them and surely, we can make it all work again... I give up quite quickly because I am sure I can't fix them but also, I am transfixed by our surroundings. Places like Westminster Abbey are fascinating to me because they are so enormous and so elaborate, and they were built in a time when everything was done by hand - the fact that buildings like this often took hundreds of years to complete is something I find rather lovely in this fast-paced, on-demand world we live in. The Sagrada Famiglia in Barcelona, designed by Gaudi still isn't finished and is probably the most incredible building I have ever stepped inside - this comes a close second.

Rowan and I are also really enjoying the organ music that is playing - Rowan is a cellist (I think she might even be a professional!) and when I was younger, as well as playing the piano, I learned to play the pipe organ too although my ability was limited to local weddings, funerals and parades and could never even come close to what we are listening to this afternoon.

As I am gazing reverently up at the roof and counting my blessings that we all made it here today, some giggling next to me tells me that the bottom has fallen out of Rich's candle as he tried to fix it and now it won't go back in - and then the penny drops - they are remote controlled candles - and they suddenly and briefly spring to life and then go out again just to prove it. I am desperate not to get the giggles (almost impossible in such an important setting) and so I smirk and look over to the seats in the Nave, as Zoe points out the back of the heads of Princess Eugenie, Princess Beatrice and Sophie Wessex - and then, as if by pure magic, we all stand as Princess Catherine, dressed in a festive red dress and matching coat and high heels (I wonder if she gets blisters) glides into view with Prince William by her side, and takes her seat almost opposite us, and the service begins.

Once in Royal David's City
Stood a lowly cattle shed,
Where a mother laid her baby,
In a manger for a bed:
Mary was that mother mild,
Jesus Christ her little child

The soloist sings, punctuating the still air of this vast, cavernous space with his perfect soprano voice, and we all glance nervously at each other with a look that silently says, 'Don't sing yet, the next verse is just the choir!'

As the glorious last notes of the last verse descant sung to perfection by the Choir of Westminster Abbey (and bringing such joy) fade into the stillness, The Very Reverend Dr David Hoyle, Dean of Westminster welcomes us all to the service while Leona Lewis takes her place in the Nave to sing 'O Holy Night' - possibly my favourite ever Christmas hymn.

As the service continues, I feel my cheeks starting to ache from all the smiling - this is such a happy and amazing occasion and to have been invited at all is such an honour. The congregation is made up of a mixture of people chosen by the country's Lord Lieutenants, who have gone above and beyond during the pandemic, and I know there are five people here from Moray, although I haven't seen them and don't know where they are sitting. We five however, are sitting in the section that has been reserved for charities that have made a difference in the last two years, as we are representing Project Wingman Foundation Ltd, the charity I founded in March 2020, using aircrew volunteers to provide well-being support to frontline NHS staff in hospital trusts across the country, and which has gone on to exceed our wildest dreams. As founder and now CEO, I oversee everything that the charity does, but it is people like Rich, Zoe, Rowan, Jack and many, many more who make things happen. Some, like Rowan and me, are no longer flying, others like Rich, Zoe and Jack all kept their jobs and are back in the air where they belong, incredibly fitting Wingman in around their work and family lives. The last two years have been nothing short of incredible, the difference we have made to people's lives both in the NHS and in our aircrew community has been astonishing, and we have been thanked and applauded by the NHS, by the government and by our industry for everything we have achieved and continue to do. I am so proud of everything we have achieved, and this year has been nothing short of incredible - a welcome light after the darkness that was 2020. Starting the year by being made MBE in the New Year Honours list and ending it sitting in Westminster Abbey at the Royal Carol Service would be incredible enough, but it has been a year that has been filled with so much more, and I am sitting here with a heart full of gratitude for all of it.

The service ends with another favourite, O Come all ye faithful, and throughout the service, I have been loving listening to a man behind me who has a very strong and very good singing voice. As we finish singing O come, let us adore him, Christ the Lord, instead of dropping to the usual last notes of Adeste Fideles the voice behind me goes up an octave and it is superb. We all turn to him and there is a little ripple of applause before we fall silent again for the blessing and the departure of the Royal party.

After everything is finished, I turn to him and tell him how much I have enjoyed his singing during the service, and we make small talk. When I turn back to my group, Jack is looking at me and says, "Do you know who that is?" I don't know who anyone is. I am completely hopeless at recognising anyone or knowing their names (Royalty aside of course) and I have no idea. I explained to Jack that I just thought he had a lovely singing voice and decided to tell him how much I enjoyed it. "That is Jason Manford," he says. I am still clueless, "Should I know who he is?" I ask Jack. It turns out that Jason Manford, owner of the fantastic singing voice, is also a well-known comedian and lives somewhere near Jack. I always feel stupid not knowing who someone is, but I also think it must be nice for people who are famous to sometimes just be spoken to like a normal person. Jason Manford, if you happen to be reading this, then I apologise for not knowing who you were at Westminster Abbey, but I really wouldn't recognise Hugh Grant if he stood in front of me with a sign saying, 'I'm Daniel Cleaver.' I promise!

Jack is desperate to say hello so I tell him to do it - you don't get these opportunities more than once after all - he tells him all about Project Wingman and asks him if he would be willing to visit our bus when it is next in Stockport - the answer is encouraging and Jason then bids us goodbye as he has to catch a train to Bedford where he has a gig that night!

We wait our turn to leave our seats and spend some happy time walking through the Abbey and taking photos - it is even more beautiful with all the Christmas Trees and the carved wooden nativity. When we have had our fill, we make our way outside where we are delighted to see the Reindeer are still, and we all enjoy petting them and taking photos - although not quite as much as Rich does - Rich, we discover, really, really likes Reindeer!

As we leave the majesty of the Abbey and tumble our way towards the nearest pub, we all reflect on what a magical time we have had that afternoon. Christmas has finally begun and the friendships we have made on Zoom calls have been firmly cemented, and toasted, and as we finally say goodbye to each other, it is not lost on any of us that we are about to enter our third year of operating a charity that has done so much for all of us, and something that none of us could ever have imagined being needed, let alone being run by people like us. This is not just my story, but the story of 6500 aircrew volunteers who chose to put themselves forward into the fray to support people they had never met before. This is the story of how Project Wingman gave people a sense of purpose in the middle of their darkest days, and how they stepped up to make other peoples lives just a little bit better.

Chapter Fifteen

7 Miles High

"Who parked it then love?" I hear for possibly the thirtieth time since I left the flight deck to say goodbye to our disembarking passengers. This might be the second most common thing passengers say to female pilots after the more traditional, and much preferred, "Thank you. Goodbye."

For some people this is irritating beyond measure - a true sign that sexism is still alive and well amongst the great British travelling public, but it has always made me giggle a bit, to be honest, and on a really good day, think of some quick reply - my favourite in response to, "Great landing love," being, "Thanks, it was my first time, I hope I get it right the next time too!" I could go on, but the point is that there are so few female airline pilots, let alone captains (you know there are four times more endangered Bengal Tigers in the world than there are female airline captains right?) When people leave one of my flights, they quite often want to say something to acknowledge this, but they don't quite know what... there is no etiquette for, 'how to greet a female airline pilot'. I get it, and I have some fun with it, especially on the rare days when I have a female co-pilot too. Even better if the flight attendants were also all women; those were the days when I welcomed people on board with 'this unmanned flight to wherever' that got people's attention, and occasionally even a round of applause; interestingly, especially from Italians - I love

Italian passengers because they clap a lot. It is quite fabulous to land as normal, at your intended destination, and hear a round of applause coming from the cabin.

I often get asked, sometimes even told, by passengers about whether or not the aircraft 'basically flies itself doesn't it?!' Actually, NO! Not at all! If it did, do you think airlines would spend as much money as they do employing two highly qualified and skilled people to sit in the flight deck? No, exactly. It is true, that we fly around a lot of the time using the built-in, sophisticated, autopilot, in Europe, it is mandated for every aircraft flying above 28,000 feet, Flight Level 280.

European airspace is busy, and so above Flight Level 280, the rules are that to maintain the correct amount of separation from other aircraft, we must have the autopilot on, or 'engaged' to use the correct terminology. With the autopilot engaged, indeed, our hands are not physically on the flight controls, and those of us who are fortunate enough to be Airbus pilots, can pull out our tray tables from beneath the screens we are constantly monitoring in front of us, and enjoy a nice, civilised breakfast, lunch, dinner, cup of tea etc., and on really long days, we may eat all three meals in the air during our duty, rather than having to balance everything on our laps. The tray table is a constant source of good-natured banter between Airbus and Boeing pilots. Boeing pilots think that Airbus pilots are slightly less worthy because we use a sidestick to control the aircraft, and our thrust levers don't physically move with thrust changes during the cruise - whereas, we Airbus pilots are smug with the knowledge that not only do we have the hallowed tray table, we also have a wider, ergonomically designed flight deck in which to spend our long days, sitting on seats which I am told were designed by Porsche.

This small room, behind its lockable bulletproof door, and with its giant windows, decorated with scores of circuit breakers, switches, screens, levers and dials, is essentially my office. It is the place where I do almost all of my work, and as well as being a different shape from an average office, the biggest difference between where you and I work is that my office is in the sky. It can be a harsh environment at times, but it always has the best views in the house, views that I never tired of. Most of the time, we are flying above the weather, so during the day, it is bright and sunny – spoiler: pilots don't wear sunglasses during the flight to 'look cool' - it is a necessity against the intense brightness of the sun. Every single day, even during the longest, darkest, wettest winter, we are above the clouds, enjoying some sunshine, even if it is through the reinforced, thickened glass of our offices in the sky. Despite the sunshine, it is very cold outside our office windows. Usually, around -62°C and although the windows are heated and we can turn the temperature in the flight deck up and down, there have been flights where my feet have been really cold - especially (but not limited to) when flying north to wonderful destinations like Keflavík (Iceland) or Tallinn (Estonia). The flight deck is reported to be dryer than Death Valley, although I have never been so haven't been able to personally compare the two, and noisy. There is engine noise, the noise of the air conditioning, in busy airspace, the noise of people talking on the radios, and the noise of a big hunk of metal (or aluminium composite) forcing its way through the air at 600 miles per hour - my headgear of choice in my office is my Bose noise cancelling headset - almost everyone who flies has one of these (other brands are available) and I never go anywhere without mine! So to summarise, I work in an office that is 6 or 7 miles up in the sky, the outside temperature is -62°C, inside it is dryer than an overcooked Christmas (or Thanksgiving) Turkey, cold at the bottom, warm at the top, separated from other people (and the loo) by a bulletproof door, and my sunglasses and battery operated noise-cancelling cans are almost permanently glued to my head - oh, and then there's night. Night time flying is actually a bit magical - it can be tiring of course, but the stars look as if they are so close you can reach out and touch them, Orion is always there, watching over us (I always used to check for him just in case!), and sometimes there are 'once in a lifetime' moments - the flight back from Malaga when we were watching a very active thunderstorm far off to our right hand side and below us, when suddenly a bolt of lightning went shooting up from the top of an enormous Cumulonimbus cloud - something that years later, my friend and colleague Marnie and I still talk about, watching the sun set over a peaceful looking world, and the moon rise, reflecting on any water it can find as it does so, and very occasionally a display of the Aurora Borealis, usually just a green glow in the distance, but on one glorious occasion, leaving Iceland, the smallest of green glimmers in the sky suddenly burst into an explosion of light and colour that lasts long enough for us to be able to tell the passengers, dim the cabin lights and perform a slow orbit so everyone gets to see them - this display is something that will stick in my memory forever, and typically, it happens on a day when my camera had run out of batteries, a 'snow leopard' moment!

Throughout my career, I have seen wonderful, and sometimes terrible things. The final sunset of a year that's about to end, or the first sunrise of a new year, catastrophic wildfires in the hills of the South of France, or Portugal, the Eiffel Tower sparkling for five minutes of every hour, the rugged coastline of Northern Spain, widespread flooding, the UK covered in snow, the smouldering wreck of a burning building in London which turned out to be the Grenfell disaster we later discovered, the snowcapped mountains of the Alps or Pyrenees, night time ski runs lit up below us, the Atlas Mountains on approach to Marrakesh, the Costa Concordia lying tragically on its side waiting to be salvaged, container ships hanging around in the north Sea waiting for the price of their cargo to rise before they go into Port to unload, the brightly coloured stripes of Tulip fields in Amsterdam, and the sun backlighting the Fresian Islands on a flight home from Tallinn.

These are all wonderful sights, and wonderful memories, a constant reminder of how small we all are in the grand masterplan of this enormous planet, but this is a happy side effect of the real reason I am sitting in my office in the first place. I am there partly for when things go wrong, that is a fact, but also because even on a 'normal' day, the aircraft can't go anywhere without me and my crew. A fully loaded A320 can weigh up to seventy-seven tons depending on the airline or configuration, and before it even gets airborne, we have overseen the loading, refuelling, safety inspections, flight plan programming, paperwork, and route clearances that take place for every single flight. We obtain permission to push back from the stand, negotiate with ground staff, organise de-icing in winter, remote holding in summer, we navigate taxi routings that can be miles long (Amsterdam, Barcelona, Madrid) and before the aircraft even moves, I have often done more 'work' than I will for the rest of the day.

I arrive at the airport in time to check in one hour before the flight is scheduled to leave and head straight for security. There is a staff channel in most airports but occasionally you have to take your chances with the rest of the passengers. Once I, and everything I am carrying with me has been screened, I meet my crew, download my flight plan onto my company-issued iPad (in the old days we used to print these off for the entire day and carry them in a brown envelope that had to be filed on our return each night), which I then check for payload (you and your luggage), weather, planned routings, weights etc and then choose how much fuel I want to take with me. Here's another myth buster: 'Low cost' airlines are not low cost when it comes to safety, and that extends to allowing the captain to choose how much fuel they need for each flight. Even on a normal day when weather conditions are expected to be good, no delays are anticipated, the aircraft is working perfectly, and there are no other considerations, a flight will always carry enough fuel to fly to its scheduled destination, be unable to land, try again, go somewhere else, and STILL land at a diversion airfield with a surplus of fuel in the tanks. It has to be this way because, unlike a car, you can't just stop and think about what to do next when you add in the third dimension of being above the ground!

The fuel figure is then relayed to the fuel delivery company, the crew are told where their aircraft is and we either walk through the terminal, or outside, along the bottom of the buildings that make up the terminal, or a bus takes us to our stand. Once there, we either take the aircraft over from another crew or open up a 'cold' aircraft but either way, the first thing that happens is lots of checking - the cabin crew checks the cabin and the pilots check the aircraft logbook, the flight deck and the outside of the aircraft to make sure everything is as it should be. By now, you will have been called to your departure gate, and will either be starting to queue up for boarding, or on a bus to come and join us, your bags are being loaded into the hold, fuel is being pumped into the fuel tanks in the wings, the aircraft has been switched on, the air conditioning is warming up the cabin on cold days and cooling it down on hot ones, we programme everything into the flight computers, calculate our performance, cross checking all the time, always checking, hopefully take a sip of coffee, check and brief the expected departure and taxi routing, checking numbers, altitudes, speeds, expectations as we go, and finally, take a breath as we watch you all walk up the steps or down the airbridge to find your seat, knowing that you are desperately hoping that you will not be sitting near that screaming child, or over excited group of teenagers, or giddy hens or stags, and the worst of all passengers - the silent 'seat kicker' (you know exactly who you are!), and just as you are all sitting down and strapping in, we speak. "Hello everyone. Welcome on board this service to Timbuktu, my name is…" etc. We know that most people don't listen but these announcements are for the benefit of the one or two people on board who do like to know that we are human beings who have names and faces, how long the flight will take, what flying conditions we are expecting and any other information that will be of benefit to the 10% of passengers who would describe themselves as 'nervous flyers'. When I became a captain, I made a deal with myself that I would always make this announcement from the front of the cabin - face to face with the people I was carrying, partly because I really loved being able to see my passengers and partly because as well as giving me an idea of the 'mood' of the 180 people who would be sitting behind me, it gave reassurance to anyone who was feeling just a bit anxious about what they were about to do. It also meant that if we were facing delays or bad weather, I could set expectations and answer questions if there were any - it just made my life and the life of my crew a bit easier.

Everything I just described takes place in the hour before the flight departs, and with the Welcome on Board announcement made, I return to my seat in the flight deck, closing the door as I go, sit down, and take a breath - it is a moment of calm and peace after a busy and noisy 60 minutes, and from now until the engines are shut down at the other end of the flight, my office is shared only with my co-pilot, usually someone different every day.

Everything that happens between this point and the point at which we engage the autopilot, happens because either me or my colleague makes it happen. The push-back off the stand, the taxi out to the holding point for our departure runway, setting the thrust, releasing the brakes as we do, roll down the runway and getting airborne, that's all done by a human being, your pilot for the day. There is no magic switch, and it won't come as any surprise at all that on the way to the runway, we are constantly checking things again. Each pilot has to check full and free movement of the flight controls, there are instruments to monitor and check and of course, the taxi routing which can be complicated, even at familiar airports like Gatwick.

There is nothing more mind-focusing and exciting than the few seconds sitting at the end of the runway, waiting for clearance, with an aircraft full of passengers sitting expectantly behind you. Clearance obtained, we advance the thrust levers, pausing to make sure each engine is running evenly, release the brakes and feel the aircraft starting to move, passing 70, 80, 90 knots, then through the point of no return, the speed known as V1, the decision speed, the point at which you must take off regardless of anything else happening, because you will be too fast to stop if you try, listening for the word 'Rotate', the signal to gently squeeze the sidestick backwards, raising the aircraft nose, and we are airborne. It doesn't matter how many times I do this; it is still a moment of magic - and then there is a lot to do as we climb away from the ground. The landing gear is retracted, we speed up, clean up the wings by retracting the flaps that we have extended to give us more lift for take-off, change radio frequency, release the cabin crew to go about their business and climb the aircraft up to its designated cruising altitude and speed. Providing it is smooth, we can switch off the seatbelt signs once we are through 10,000 feet, and then, maybe, there is a moment to take another sip of by now cold coffee. By the time we have been at work for two hours we will often be at our cruise altitude, or very close to it, where we will have time to sit and plan our approach at our destination, and on a long flight, maybe even pull out a newspaper or magazine (but never a book!)

The beginning and end of every flight demands a high workload, but the bit in the middle is often very quiet, and there is always room for humour in our jobs. I have never known if it is a coping mechanism for the hours we work, a way of releasing a portion of the enormous weight of responsibility we carry around with us, or the fact that we spend a large part of our lives, in a small space with someone we don't know well, but I have spent my fair share of time laughing at work. Almost everything can be funny with the right person. It might be listening to a very pompous captain trying to barge his way up the de-icing queue like no one else has somewhere they need to be, or even funnier, refusing to accept that he has to wait for anything at all (never argue with Air Traffic Control - they have your life in their hands). Taxi instructions in Amsterdam are always funny if a preceding aircraft happens to be a Fokker (I will leave the rest of that to your imagination) or it might be the name of a waypoint or group of waypoints. All flights operate along imaginary highways in the sky called airways, and they run between specified locators called Waypoints. Sometimes these are actual places - it might be an airport or a geographical feature, but sometimes waypoints are given other names. RODNI for example is reported to be overhead the Only Fools and Horses actor David Jason's house in London, whilst UVAVU is overhead the home of Vic Reeves in the Northeast of England in a nod to 1990s quiz show Shooting Stars. There are also slightly dodgy and even rude waypoints - and yes, I have looked them all up! WANKA, DIKAS and COQUE are favourites, there is a routing out over the Bay of Biscay that takes you from RUBMI to TITUB and then on to COQUE, there are two BOLOX in the world (you will be relieved to hear) and Spanish ATC frequently gets fed up with pilots who are asked to route to Robledillo or RBO reading it back as Rubber Dildo. You see, the other side to our extreme professionalism, and high level of training and checking, is that innate need to let off steam, and if that is seeing the funny side of waypoints in the course of the day, I'm a fan! There are other waypoints of course, that also make up some good routings. I once heard that down the eastern seaboard of the US, there were four waypoints named MARY, HADA, LIDL and LAMB, at high-level overhead Essex you can find STOAT, WESUL and FERIT, with TUNEL being located over the Dartford Crossing. VASUX in the English Channel is reportedly named after a Virgin Atlantic aircraft that encountered a problem on departure and had to fly up and down the channel burning fuel to become light enough to land, severely disrupting air traffic for hours and causing long delays - who said the department that names waypoints doesn't have a sense of humour?!

The best routing however has to be one to the north of Munich which goes GIVMI-WISKY-INBED - summing up exactly how we all feel late at night before seeing the lights of Belgium which signal the start of the descent into Gatwick and therefore the end of a long day!

Whilst taking off is something only the pilots can do, landing is slightly different. Most landings are conducted manually by one or other of the pilots, but there is one exception, and that is when it is foggy. Some airports have the right equipment to allow a crew to perform an autoland. For the pilots to carry out a landing, there has to be enough of a visual reference, we have to be able to see the runway we are landing on - that makes sense right - but what about the days when we can't? Well, if you are heading for somewhere like my local airport of Inverness in the fog, you can expect to divert somewhere else, but if you are heading to a larger and busier airport, it is possible to programme the aircraft to land without the pilots having to see anything at all. This is a highly monitored, extremely intense approach because we have to be ready to intervene and perform a go-around at any point (the same is true of all approaches but in this case, we would have to take over from the machine). During my career, this was something I had to do on a small number of occasions, and you have to trust that the aircraft is going to do the right thing. You will know if an autoland is going to be carried out because a special announcement will be made asking you to switch all electronic devices fully off rather than just have them in airplane mode, and it is a wonder of modern aviation that it is even possible. It is something we train for and practice in every simulator session, and I remember clearly after the first time I had to do this for real in the aircraft as captain, how empowering it was to carry out this type of approach, trusting my knowledge and ability as much as the capability of the aircraft, and it all working out as it should, and remembering the golden rule which is NEVER to tell your colleague that you are doing something for the first time! There can be no chink in the armour!

An autoland, will often, but not always be the end of a long day in the office, and once we have parked the aircraft on its designated stand, you gather your things together and make your way to your final destinations while we switch off screens and lights, plug-in ground power and switch off the small engine at the back of the aircraft (called the Auxiliary Power Unit or APU), unplug our headsets, pack our belongings into our flight bags, and as captain, I was always the last to leave the aircraft, switching off the lights as I went and closing the door, often knowing that in twelve hours, I would be back to do it all again. No matter how long the day has been, or what challenges we have overcome during it, I would always walk down the steps and away from the aircraft feeling proud of a job well done, having delivered my passengers all over Europe, and would look forward to whatever the next duty would bring, never boring, a different aircraft, different weather, different destinations, different passengers and different colleagues. Always the same, but always different.

Do I miss commercial flying? Absolutely. Would I change anything? Well, apart from the way 'lockdown' brought that part of my career to an unexpected and abrupt halt and nearly killed the airline industry, no, I wouldn't. As I have attempted to illustrate throughout this book, life is punctuated by moments that challenge you; it is how you react to those moments that not only demonstrates your mettle, but is where you find out who you are, what your core values are, and what your purpose is. These are the times when you grow the most. Within those moments I gained enormous strength from amazing people that did not hesitate to step up and help; some were asked and did not even blink while saying yes, some did not have to be asked, they just reached out and stepped up. When I think of how colleagues across the airline industry came together to help each other, and those in the NHS, when needed most, I don't mind admitting it brings a tear of admiration to the eye, but also makes me well up with pride. At my lowest points and through the toughest of days, I have been deeply moved by the generosity of spirit in others. All it takes for positive change to break through, is for good people to do good things for someone else, and in that paying it forward, the very best of human nature will win through.

We each have the possibility within us to change the world for the better, and one way we can do that is to strive to make a difference within the corner of the world we inhabit. All we need to do is be bold enough to keep throwing the pebbles into the pond, the ripples will do the rest.

The End... *of the beginning*